My 5 Minutes in Heaven

How It Could Happen to You

MARK MAGILL

Fulton Books
Meadville, PA

Published by Fulton Books 2024

ISBN 979-8-89221-375-2 (paperback)
ISBN 979-8-89427-387-7 (hardcover)
ISBN 979-8-89221-376-9 (digital)

Unless otherwise noted, all Scripture quotations are taken from the Complete Jewish Bible. Copyright © 1998. Used by permission.

Bold and italics in scripture quotations reflect the author's emphasis.

Printed in the United States of America

To Adonai, Jesus, and the Holy Spirit, to whom I am eternally
grateful for their direct interventions in my life in part and in whole
To Mom, who tried to understand me and the experiences
God gave me throughout His complex plan for my life

*Come and listen, all you who fear God,
and I will tell you what He has done for me.
I cried out to Him with my mouth,
His praise was on my tongue.
Had I cherished evil thoughts,
Adonai would not have listened.
But in fact, God did listen;
He paid attention to my prayer.
Blessed be God, who did not reject my prayer
or turn His grace away from me.*

—Psalm 66:16–20 CJB

CONTENTS

INTRODUCTION

At the age of two, I was in the hospital with a bump on my forehead. Two boys had been chasing me around a VW bus while I was looking over my shoulder. When I looked ahead, my forehead hit the front chrome bumper, and I was out cold. Such accidents are dangerous for a child at a young age but can also bring about a deeper insight into the realm of the supernatural. The army had a special team to recruit just such people for their *Green Lantern Project.*

When I was an atheist at the age of ten, I had no hope for the future. Just to keep going from one day to the next was a struggle. There were no dreams for the future, no hope for a better tomorrow, just a plodding shuffle from one day to the next with no groups of friends with whom to share experiences. The television was my babysitter.

I was a latchkey kid who was being brought up by a socialist secular system that did not really care and was passed along from one classroom to another. No teaching of Christ or the Bible was ever mentioned in any of those classes. I threw caution to the wind, becoming interested in the supernatural realm and experimenting with it. It was dangerous but fascinating as I started to look around the corner of the wall of death—come what may. That is when my life became a wild and crazy series of supernatural adventures, one after another.

Years later, the only logical choice was to put my faith into Christ and start reading the Bible, with the Holy Spirit making sure I read and accepted every page as truth. This was after Christ himself put his hand on me and corrected me. Then the cracked foundation of my self-made religion exploded, and the whole ramshackle structure collapsed. What then came was a flawless foundation built on solid rock with a perfect cornerstone, on which was being built a new structure made of gold, silver, and precious stones, not the wood, rope, and iron beams surrounded by walls of black bricks that I had been using to create my own religious skyscraper.

Metaphorically speaking, while you are an unbeliever, God has his back to you, and you have your back to him. *You* have to be brave and make the first move by declaring that God is there.

Writing this book is what I owe to God, for I am finally doing what he has in mind to help the world grasp on to his life plan of hope and redemption. This is where God in his infinite wisdom has placed me in the center of the debates of what death is, who God is, where He is, how you are brought up to heaven or down to hell, and why the Bible is the key to all truth. God has shown me amazing things, by breaking the unbiblical religious rules of our day, like asking God for what you are "not supposed to" ask him for, and that is what I will be doing for you in this book, to apply them to your life and perhaps get your five minutes—or more—in heaven in a pre-rapture, or the full rapture, experience.

From the age of ten, I had compared the Bible to a telephone book, as it was too large and cumbersome to bother reading. I was not an avid reader by any means, though I did read the classics and a few novels. My routine dismissive attitude of the Bible and being an honest doubter are two of the reasons God had chosen me to have an experience from him first, and then hours, days, months, or years later, it would be revealed to me in his Word as a confirmation that the Bible is the highest level of truth and everything else is varying degrees of deception.

One of the earliest of these experiences as an atheist was when I met up with a rich man in hell, and it exactly compares to the parable Jesus himself gave of the poor man in Abraham's bosom and the rich man in hell. Likewise, I could not explain what I had seen in my five minutes in heaven until after I read Revelations 21 and 22 nine years later.

I am writing this book from the perspective of a fully convinced Christian looking back on all the gifts and personal corrections God has given to me over the years. I have been through occultism, atheism, Buddhism, agnosticism, and New Ageism, animal spirit guided meditations, past-life regression, and near-death yoga for astral projection in that order, starting at the age of ten.

None of them prepared me for what I saw in the actual heaven or even gave me a glimpse into the one true God who knows each one of us down to our very thoughts. I am writing this book to exegete the Bible, not to eisegete it.

When it comes to out-of-body experiences, I have been very careful to only stay within the realms of God's intent and usage of our OOB adventures because I have been taught by a fellowship how to go into a form of self-induced near-death experience through breath control that is not in the Bible. This ended in demon possession, which, by Christ's own hand, was itself pulled out of me and dropped into the pit of hell. So in this book, I include biblical events that can be clearly defined as moments of being "in the spirit."

None of the listed accounts and recollections in this book are fiction. These are all factual events that could not be concocted by even the wildest imagination because I refer each experience to the Bible. The Bible will stand true today even in a court of law, as there are over five hundred attested witnesses listed therein. I do not need to defend the Bible, as I do not need to defend a charging lion. I reiterate God gives to me the experience first, then I later find it in the Bible. One of my objectives in this book is to present the thought process of an unbeliever to help with the development of apologetics.

My hope is that this book will bring about a step-by-step understanding of what is really going on in the spiritual background of everyday life. I want to help you and others see what is possible to experience while you are still here on earth.

I will include my five minutes in heaven and an actual map of the things I had seen there with approximate locations and distances from the south central of the twelve pearl gates to the New Jerusalem, God's Beryl Throne, and the Tree of Life. While I was an atheist in the army ROTC, I had learned map reading and how to plot a course.

My hope is that you will come to know Christ and the Bible in full measure and to be baptized for evidence of your faith before all mankind. Welcome to your new adventure in life. There is no turning back now.

CHAPTER 1
Wide Is the Path

I was sitting in a semi-lotus position in front of a small prayer table that was laden with a collection of carefully chosen polished stones: a bloodstone, a dark purple amethyst with white rings, a hematite, and a large quartz crystal. A small candle was flickering in the center. My bedroom door and windows were locked—there was no one else in the room. Recalling the unusual day, I reflected on what my coworker had said.

It was still morning, and we were disassembling a huge semiconductor robotic workstation for shipment, and I was the tool owner. He said suddenly, "I'm studying to be an Assembly of God pastor. So what do you believe in?"

"Well, I believe that God is on the other side of the universe and through meditation, you can achieve a higher state of mind so as to reach the pinnacle of human existence, or self-realization." He stared at me in amazement, so I fell silent.

"My friend, I want you to do two things for me," he said.

"What are they?"

"Ask God if what you have been taught is the truth, and ask Jesus into your heart."

"You're on! My religion is against yours." My thoughts returned to the candle on the prayer table. I quietly sang a song the fellowship had taught me, "Door of My Heart, Open Wide I keep for Thee."

The fellowship I had belonged to in California had taught me to send a *soul call* to God, a simple prayer laden with genuineness that came straight from the heart. And once it was sent to God, who was on the other side of the universe, the fellowship told me, "You were to keep the 'door of your heart' open and receptive to the impending reply." I even had the door of my heart wide open for Christ to walk into; he did not even have to knock. He could just come in and sup with me.

As I sat there alone in my bedroom, I poured all my love for God into a golden ball with the simple message that I had prepared as a *soul call*. "Lord God," I said, "I ask you if what I have been taught is the truth and ask Jesus into my heart." Then I launched the golden message sphere like a rocket to God, from my heart directly to him on the other side of the universe. I was confident that I would receive an overwhelming feeling of love from God that I was indeed in the right, as was my experience with God so many times before.

But this time, there was no reply, no overwhelming feeling of love and justification, nothing. Then I realized that it was time for me to go to bed, as it was late and I had to get up early for work. Instead, I straightened my back and stiffened my neck. *No,* I thought, *I am going to sit here till I get an answer!*

The moment I had finished that thought, a hand gripped my right shoulder from behind. I knew it was Jesus Christ himself, standing right behind me. He was King of kings and Lord of lords, and that was not to be questioned.

I was so stunned I could not even turn to look at him. He leaned over and said into my right ear, "You have been lied to," and then he let go of my right shoulder and was gone.

A vision quickly overtook me, and I was looking down on a land of skyscrapers from a height of three hundred feet and saw a dark tower standing below. It was made of black beams—some were wood, some steel, and all held together by rope and rivets. The outer walls were of black brick.

I saw an explosion go off at the foundation of the dark tower, and the entire structure quickly came crashing down. I was devastated because I knew it represented my self-made religion. Then I became angry because as Jesus himself had just said, I had been lied to for over eighteen years by the world.

I blew out the candle and put away the collection of polished stones. Then I reached to the upper shelf in the closet and pulled out a King James Version Bible that was given to me by a prolific Seventh-Day Adventist preacher, Lyle Albrecht. I sat there and started reading that Bible for the first time, starting with Genesis. I was rather disgruntled having to read it, but I knew full well that after Christ put his hand on my shoulder, the Bible was the only source of truth, and everything else was varying degrees of deception.

*****

Back in high school, my best friend, Willie, and I were biking along the sidewalk on our ten speeds, in front of a FedMart shopping center. We played AD&D together quite often. He was a Christian who went to a local church.

"What do you believe happens after you die?" he said.

"Well," I began, "it's like turning off a TV set. The whole screen goes blank, and that's it."

"You believe that? That's sad."

I was perplexed at his response that he did not believe the same thing I did.

Four years earlier in middle school, I was listening to the seventh-grade science teacher as she told us the theory of how life began. She drew on the chalkboard all the levels of a pond, from the surface down the ooze layer.

"On the surface of a pond is duckweed and such," she began. "Then, there's the water layer, where fish live and die. Then, on the bottom, there's the ooze layer, where fish poop and dead animals collect. Life began when two tiny amoeba bubbled up from the ooze layer and began mutating after the pond was struck by lightning." Then she showed us the evolutionary chart of how animals and humans evolved. At the age of twelve, I was intrigued by her instruction as I had never heard such things before.

*****

Through the early enlistment program, I had joined the Air Force to become an HVAC and power production specialist. Getting ready to head south to the San Diego airport, I kissed my mother goodbye and stepped into my red 1973 Firebird Esprit, and the 350cc V8 engine roared to life.

While stationed at Minot AFB, I often surfed the channels on cable TV in my dorm room. I watched a pre-recorded show of Billy Graham on one of his evangelist tours and was intrigued but was indifferent to his preaching. On that Sunday, a fellow airman had invited me to go to his church, and I agreed. After the services were over, the entire congregation was instructed to shake hands and say, "Peace to you." I shook hands with him, and he said, "Peace to you!"

I recalled a line from an old joke and said, "Peace on you too!"

Watching a CNN news exclusive on out-of-body experiences, I went to visit my favorite bookstore at the Dakota Square Mall. While at B. Dalton Books, I found a book on astral projection and purchased it. Having studied Nostradamus while in high school, I also bought a book that entailed all his quatrains, listed side by side in French and English, along with the possible revelations from the future according to planetary alignment. There was one quatrain in which he listed the three devices he used for divination, and I found that one interesting. In one interview I watched on CNN, there was a man talking about a book called the *Necronomicon*, and I was intrigued.

As I approached the Dakota Square mall, I noticed a Christian bookstore near the entrance and walked past it, sneering. I found the B. Dalton bookstore and purchased a black copy of the *Necronomicon* in paperback. The cashier looked at me funny. Back on base, I read through the entire book and was curious about the snake people in the desert, the *Mad Arab* mentioned with great fear and trepidation. The rest of the book was a meh, except for the last pages that mentioned spiritual gateways and how to open them. That gave me an idea.

While walking around that bookstore again, I saw a book on astral projection and opened it. I was intrigued by its possibilities, bought it, and studied it on base. Reading about how to engage in out-of-body travel through astral projection proved to be quite a challenge. Lying quietly on the bed and performing breath control was already a challenge. But trying to channel your awareness *out* of your physical body through a metaphysical well in the region of your solar plexus and then up into your mirror image of a supernatural body that was hovering just a few feet above you was quite another. As hard and as often as I tried, I could not get my awareness to go up the funnel.

When the time came to leave the Minot and the Active Duty Air Force for the California Air National Guard, I packed my duffel bag into the Firebird and started the long trip home to California. Along the way, I stopped in Las Vegas for an overnight stay. Because of reading a book of tricks on how to play the slots, I continued the trip the next day with some extra cash.

My first assignment with the new unit in the California Air Guard was to send me on a trip to Keesler AFB, near Biloxi, Mississippi. Once there, I was taught on how to maintain digital radio systems, thus continuing my education in electronics, telecommunications, and computer logic.

While staying in an NCO dorm called *The Locker House*, I was playing pool one evening with another sergeant in the recreation room. In the middle of the game, the NCO grabbed the eight ball and said, "Do you believe in God?"

I was stunned. "I don't know…I'm not sure," I replied. He handed me a pamphlet on how to meditate the Zen Buddhist way. I put the pamphlet into the upper right pocket of my uniform.

Alone in my dorm room, I sat in a semi-lotus position and focused on disciplining my thoughts for the first time. Every time a random thought would come into the forefront of my mind, I would push it out. This continued until I was able to sit there for an hour and a half with no thoughts at all. Then a wave of bliss washed over me, and it was very peaceful.

When graduation day came and went, I stuffed my duffel bag into the back seat of the Firebird and left Keesler for the last time. While cruising along Highway 10, I noticed how the swamplands and humidity of Louisiana gradually changed to the scrublands of Texas. Continuing on from Texas came the deserts of New Mexico with the tall dark extinct volcanoes and then passed along the tall cacti in Arizona. I suddenly realized that the world could not have been created by accident, as the change was so perfectly gradual from one environment to another.

*****

Arriving back in San Diego and starting a new job in information systems, I became bored with meditating the Buddhist way. Looking for a church to join, I was handed a pamphlet that had quite a different message. As I read it one night in my bedroom, one phrase stuck with me: "Take the lion's leap of faith and believe in God."

I was alone in my bedroom, and the door was locked. Kneeling in front of my bed, I said, "Is there a god, or isn't there a god? Is there a god, or isn't there a god? Is there a god, or isn't there a god? Is there a god, or isn't there a God?" And then it clicked. It made logical sense: the long trip back from Mississippi and taking in the gradual changes in the organized natural landscape as I drove past it all. There had to be a God to create a planet whose environment flowed together so coherently. So I stood up, clenched my fists to my chest, and said, "God, you're there!"

A black hole opened in my ceiling, and through it, God said, "Yes, I AM!"

Fear took over my heart, and then the porthole between heaven and earth quickly closed up. I was in awe that he had responded to me directly, for I had been told by the fellowship that God was a force of energy on the other side of the universe who was vaguely aware of your existence. I was surprised to find out that God knew exactly who I was and where I was, but I did not know why he responded to me in anger.

CHAPTER 2
My Five Minutes in Heaven

Two weeks later, while working in the information systems company, I reflected on how God had revealed himself to me and that his voice was so full of authority, it was frightening. At home, I was shocked and amazed that he was willing to speak to a person directly, for I had never heard of such a thing happening before. He spoke with absolute authority, and I knew that he was real. His yelling through the darkness at me was frightening, much like an angry father. But the fellowship said that God never became angry at anyone, and I wondered why they were wrong on that account.

I also knew that he would hear my prayers and that I could rely on him to answer my questions. But I still did not want to read the Bible, even though the fellowship church sold the King James Version in the gift shop along with Hindu idols. The Bibles were high up on the top shelf, but the idols were on a low table, easy to reach. I looked at a cast brass statue of an elephant-man god that was very well made and thought about it.

Then, I remembered in a middle school metal shop how we made cast aluminum horse heads, camp cookers, and other such things. Then I realized all the statues of gods were made of aluminum, iron, or brass in a foundry. I could never worship a statue because it was made of earthly materials. What would be the point?

In my defiant ignorance of that time, I bought neither a statue nor a Bible. This was because when I was an atheist, I swore I would never have anything to do with Christ or the Bible, and I had compared the Bible to a telephone book. Who would want to read through a telephone book from beginning to end?

Then, a new thought entered into my mind. I wondered about what heaven must be like. The New Age religion told me that once you were in heaven, you could manipulate light rays to create anything you want. The media was always pushing the idea of meeting St. Peter at the pearly gates and waiting in line with everyone else, hoping that you had done enough good works to enter. But which version was correct?

So while I was at work, I decided that when I got home that evening, I would ask the only one I knew who could separate fact from fiction. That night, I humbled myself before the heavenly Father, and from the bottom of my heart, I gave him all my love without condition and then asked him to show me what heaven was like. After waiting patiently for what seemed like hours, I became aware that he did receive my prayer, but was not going to reply. I thanked him for listening to me, got up from my semi-lotus position, and went to bed.

Then, while I was at work again, it hit me. My desire for money was greater than my desire for a relationship with God, and I was deeply saddened at my discovery.

When I reached home that afternoon, I knew what I had to do. At home in my bedroom and fully engrossed in meditation, I sent a heartfelt message—or soul call as the fellowship called it—to the Lord my God. According to the fellowship, you put your question to God into a golden bubble as a gift and wrap it with love and then launch it out like a catapult from your heart directly to him to receive it on the other side of the universe.

In my *soul call*, I let God know that I had cast down my desire for money and then placed him first. I wrapped the prayer with love and then sent it to the other side of the universe, until I was breathless.

I waited expectantly for a familiar feeling of fulfilling peace that he had touched me with so many times before, telling me that he had received my prayer of a visit to heaven, and it would be answered. I waited a long time in absolute silence, but there was no reply, nothing at all, even though I knew very well that he had received my prayer.

The next day was a Friday, and the work was easy. There was no overtime scheduled for Saturday and no National Guard duty, so it looked as though I would have the weekend to myself.

But deep inside, I felt unable to shake the fact that there was something I was overlooking, something that was in my heart was preventing the heavenly Father from answering my soul call. *What else could be stopping him from answering me?* I thought, *Maybe I haven't done enough good deeds?*

When I was at home, I assumed the semi-lotus position and then went deeply into meditation in my bedroom. I opened my heart to him and suddenly realized that good deeds did nothing but promote me in the eyes of others and did nothing to glorify God.

Remembering a family trip to Tijuana when I was nine, I recalled how we were walking along a dirty street while I was holding tightly onto my mother's hand. We walked past an old woman wearing a black robe who was sitting on the ground and begging for money with a paper cup. I dug into my right pocket and fished out all the money I had—one quarter. I ran to the old woman and saw that she was blind in her right eye. With a smile, I quickly dropped my quarter into her cup. She shook the cup and mumbled something.

Another thing I remembered was when I was stationed in Minot AFB, North Dakota. I drove my maintenance team through the blinding snow of a blizzard to get to a remote government facility that was out of power. With a windchill factor of sixty-six degrees below zero, my crew and I noticed a yellow 19'77 Trans Am stranded on the side of the road. We pulled over to make sure that no one was inside. Wearing an Arctic parka, pants, and boots, I walked through the freezing winds of the Siberian Express and peered into the window. I saw a young man, his wife, and their six-year-old daughter sitting inside—none of them were wearing anything more than summer clothes. The car's battery was dead, and so we jump-started their engine and then followed them until they were safely on their way home.

There were a great many other good deeds that I had done as well. So I looked up toward heaven and then lifted up my good works before God, saying, "See here, Lord! These are all the good things that I have done—up to this very moment!" With all my might, I threw them down to the ground and smashed them into pieces. Then, I stomped them into the ground until they were dust. I yelled out, "There is nothing I can do to impress you, Lord! All of my good deeds do nothing but promote myself!" Then I wept bitterly.

When I regained my composure, I looked up and said to him, "Although I have done nothing to deserve it, please let me see heaven." After I had waited a long time with no reply, I began to fall into despair. As I stood there in silence, my hopes began to fade as time passed with no reply and no gentle touch of acknowledgment from him, nothing.

Then a feeling of weakness worked its way up my legs, and my knees began to shake. I fell to my knees, threw my hands up into the air, and with tears in my eyes, cried out, "Lord God, in the name of your Son, Jesus, I beg you to let me see heaven! Just give me five minutes!"

Before I could say another word, there was a loud *bang* that went off like a thunderclap right in front of my face. His voice was angry, and he shouted, "BE YOU STILL! And be prepared to receive a gift from heaven that your body *cannot* contain!"

I trembled with fear, as his angry voice demanded attention. I was so terrified by his command that I was unable to move. All I could do was to wait while kneeling before my chest of drawers and see what he was going to do to me. I could sense a vast supernatural power swirling around my room. It was as if I was in the eye of an unseen, spirit-swarming hurricane.

I wanted to know what was happening and felt compelled to look up. When I did, the ceiling in my room rolled back like a scroll, and I was staring up into the night sky. The sky was so clear that I could count all the stars. I could see the tops of the surrounding trees in the neighborhood. I then noticed a small dark cloud forming high in the sky about the size of a man's thumb, with a funnel shape pro-truding from the bottom of it. The cloud began to grow quickly, and as I watched, the funnel worked its way downward toward the earth. As I stared at the funnel, I noticed that it altered its course slightly and increased in speed.

My only thought was, *It's heading toward this neighborhood.* Observing its progress, I could see that the mouth of it was heading toward my house. As it drew closer, I saw that the mouth of it was coming toward my room. As the whirlwind began to skim the treetops, it had gained so much power that I felt as if it were a freight train going full speed and the mouth of it was headed right for me.

When the mouth of that funnel hit me, I was suddenly blasted off my feet and soared straight up—filled with absolute joy. I continued to rocket straight up and up at an incredible rate of speed while wearing only a light robe.

When I had reached a very great height, I slowed to a sudden stop. I was hovering with my arms out and feet straight down as if I were on a cross and held aloft by some unseen force. There was a light-blue sky all around me, and the striated cirrus cloud layer was just beneath my feet.

All I could think was, *Whatever God has in mind for me.* At that moment, I drifted forward. On the horizon, I could see a light-brown wall in the distance. It was very long and very tall and had three enormous pearls lodged into it: one on the left, one on the right, and one in the middle.

As I drifted toward it, I could see the brown stone wall had three large gateways blocked by enormous pearls, and each one was at least ten feet in diameter. Drifting toward the center pearl, I kept my mind and heart open toward *whatever God had in mind for me,* so I *drifted* through it. When I was on the other side, I came to a stop, and then my feet touched the ground.

As I looked on, the first thing I noticed was that at a distance of fifty feet, hundreds of people in white robes were walking to the left and right—with an expression of absolute delight on their faces. With their hands gently crossed over their chests, they were all looking upward at the light-blue sky as they walked. On occasion, I observed that one or two of the people would suddenly stop and thrust their hands into the air and shout some joyful thing three times, but I could not hear them. Then I noticed that none of the people could see or hear me. They were totally unaware of my presence, as I could not enter into heaven more than thirty yards just beyond the center pearl gate.

As soon as I noticed the outline of some golden houses and a temple in the background, which resembled those in ancient Jerusalem, I was turned to the right, and my attention was quickly snatched away by an enormous, magnificent tree reaching all the way up into the light-blue sky. It was about a half of a mile away, in a shallow green valley and in the middle of a river.

The tree's branches stretched incredibly far; its trunk was white, and its millions of huge leaves were round and as large as dinner plates. They shimmered green and gold—green on one side and gold on the other. I wanted to see just how tall the tree really was and focused on the trunk of the tree and then began to lean back while casting my eyes upward. While keeping in mind where the trunk was, I looked up and up and up and then noticed that angels in light-blue robes were flying up to the branches of the tree with empty hands. When they left the tree and drifted downward, their arms were laden full with many kinds of fruit and dropped them to the people below. My feet were firmly planted on the ground at the entrance, and I was unable to approach the tree. It was as if I was standing fast on a potter's wheel, which was being turned left and right by an unseen force.

As I stood there staring at the tree, I felt a small tug at the base of my spine, and a thought came into my mind, *It's time for you to go home.*

"That can't be," I replied. "I am home! I'm with the Lord!" I was turned to the right and faced a brilliant bluish-white light. I threw my hands straight into the air and cried out, "Praise Adonai! Praise Yeshua! Praise be to the Ruach HaKodesh!" I was so overtaken by a fulfilling power and tremendous joy as I praised them as one that a powerful energy suddenly swept *up* through my body, flowing up into my feet and then surging its way upward through the top of my head, slowly lifting me off the ground as I glorified God three times.

When I stopped praising him and the energy released me, my feet touched the ground, and I was turned to the left to see the wonderful tree again. Gazing at the center, I started to look for the top of it again and leaned so far back that I was almost looking straight up.

Still, I could not see the top of it. I felt another tug at the small of my back, and a thought came into my mind saying, *If you do not return to your earthly body, it will die.* My smile grew, and I said, "I don't care! It doesn't matter! I am at home with the Lord!"

I was turned to the right, I threw my hands straight into the air, and while I faced the brilliant bluish-white light again, I saw the right armrest and back left foot of a greenish-white stone throne. I cried out, "Praise Adonai! Praise Yeshua! Praise be to the Ruach HaKodesh!" The same wonderful, powerful energy swept through my body again, slowly lifting me off my feet as I glorified God before his throne.

I turned my attention to the wonderful tree once again. I started to look for the top of it, and while looking straight up, I still could not see the top of it. I felt the tug again at the small of my back, and this time I heard, "It is the Lord's desire that you should return, for your life on earth is not yet complete."

My joy faltered for a moment, and while I gazed up at that beautiful tree one last time, I quietly said, "Then not my will but his will be done."

I was suddenly yanked out of the heavenly place, and my spiritual body slammed head first into the chest of my earthly body, and I gasped. I was sitting in a semi-lotus position and felt as though my face was glowing. I was still filled with that powerful joy, but it was fading. In my reflection on the window to my right, I could see that my face was glowing the same bluish-white light that I had seen in heaven, but the light emanating from me was also fading. I pressed the palms of my hands onto my face and realized that it was wet from tears of experiencing a perfect happiness.

My T-shirt was soaked with them. All the time that I was there, I had no thoughts or memories of anything that had happened on earth. I had briefly thought of planet earth for a moment while I was there but shook it off. I didn't even want to remember my life on earth, for the joy was so great.

CHAPTER 3
Why Me?

While stationed at Minot AFB, an AD&D friend from San Diego sent me a *Hagar the Horrible* comic strip. He was shipwrecked and cried to the heavens, "Why me?"

God said to him from a dark cloud above, "Why not you?"

One answer is that God chooses the losers, the lonely, and the isolated. When I was seven, my mother and father were divorced, and he even took the car, leaving a mother with three children, who had no income and no transportation. Even so, my sisters and I would wait for him at the corner of a convenience store so that he would pick us up for our weekend visit. Then, one Saturday morning, after waiting for him a very long time, my eldest sister said, "He's not coming. Let's go."

I did not know it, but my heart was hardening with a deep hatred of my father for abandoning us. But unbeknownst to me, this is when God took mercy on us and started to give me blessings despite my unbelief. For even though my mother with three kids was abandoned by her husband, essentially becoming a widow, she was able to get an apartment at first by getting three jobs using only a bicycle. A year later, we were given a condo to live rent-free for twelve years. In Psalm 68, it says:

> God in His holy dwelling is a father to orphans and defender of widows. God gives homes to those who are alone and leads prisoners out into prosperity. But rebels must live in a parched wasteland.

My father was a mocker of God and a drinker of wine, to quote from Proverbs. While my mother and father were married, there were a lot of fights every night. As I recall, the fighting started early one night. I walked down to the first landing of the stairs and looked down the last flight and into the kitchen. My father was pulling on my mother's leg as she held desperately onto the door frame of the pantry. Ninety percent of all domestic abuse starts with the man, and it usually involves money, alcohol, pride, and jealousy. Every six seconds in this country, a woman is abused by a husband or a significant other.

My dreams were filled with dread, the first one being in a boat moving slowly down a dark tunnel. My best friend, his father, and I looked to the left wall of the tunnel to see a window display of two skeletons, one in a groom's tuxedo and the other in a wedding dress. This was a prophetic dream predicting the death of my mother's and father's marriage.

The next dream I had took place in a doctor's surgical room. A headless, armless, and legless body wearing only a white T-shirt and tighty-whities was on a gurney and frantically bouncing around the room, trying to escape. The doctor looked exasperated. The interpretation is that the body was me, unable to express myself and trapped in a situation I could not escape from no matter which way I turned.

In the third dream at the age of seven, I was buried six feet under in a dark-gray suit and lying in a casket. I could see my mother, father, and sisters on the surface grieving over me, and I cried too. Then my father woke me up and said, "Why are you crying?"

I said, "Daddy, I was dead! I was dead!" He held me close, and we cried together. Death in a dream is symbolic of a forthcoming huge change in your life. Once again, divorce was imminent. That house where all this happened was on Mount Alifan in the Pacific Bluffs townhomes, located in San Diego. Dreams are from God to let us know what is going on presently and in the future, as it says in Acts 2:17:

ADONAI says: "In the Last Days, I will pour out from my Spirit upon everyone. Your sons and

daughters will prophesy, your young men will see
visions, your old men will dream dreams."

These were the beginnings of a life alone with no father and with few or no friends. In Genesis 2:18, God said, "It is not good for a man to be alone." One of the reasons for God the Father saying this is that when a man is left to his own devices, he may delve into the things of the supernatural due to the length of time on his hands. He will often ponder into testing things like Balaam and Nostradamus. They both practiced divination and delved into the world of the supernatural.

God talked to Balaam because Balaam was a descendant of Abraham and had learned things that mankind was not meant to know. Through supernatural delving, Balaam drew God's attention and came to know the Lord directly. He lived near Haran where Abraham grew up, a remote backwater four hundred miles away from the nearest city. Balaam was not part of the community of Israel, but he had come to know the living God nonetheless—me too.

The way I came to know the Lord God Adonai was when I declared my total faith and acceptance that he was the creator of the world because the natural world is clearly organized. What I did not know was that when I clung to him with all my heart and said, "God, you're there!", he opened up a portal between heaven and earth to say to me, "Yes, I AM!"

This was a correction and a connection from the throne room in heaven down to me. God will judge the unbelievers who love nature but still cling to the false notion that it was all created by accident, also known as the Big Bang theory, which will always remain just that—a theory.

That is because the first law of thermodynamics states that *energy can neither be created nor destroyed.* God has always been in the spirit, which is the purest form of energy, and his purest source has created the universe or the multiverse.

I was amazed at how Hollywood got it right when they revealed the movie *Dr. Strange.* The first fifteen minutes of that movie showed him opening portals to another dimension. When God opened the portal between heaven and earth to yell at me to my face, I knew he was the Father to be feared and obeyed.

As I saw the gradual change in the environment, it became obvious that all things in nature were not created by accident. The first law of thermodynamics states that *energy can neither be created nor destroyed; it can only be transferred from one form to another.* The energy that created the universe came from God's mouth, and from there, all creation came into existence. The Big Bang theory tries to claim that the universe came into existence from nothing and then there was an explosion. Law trumps theory every time because whether by the calculator or in a controlled environment, it is a proven scientific fact.

I find it interesting that no person I have ever heard of had asked God for a visit to heaven. I was willingly ignorant of the Bible at the time I asked, and I had no reason to not ask. As such, I bargained down to five minutes in heaven, and it was not given to me until I destroyed all my good works and asked, or begged rather, in Jesus's name. My first step that week was to consciously overturn my love for money over God. After all, God created all wealth.

In Matthew 7:7 Jesus said:

> Keep on asking, and you will receive what you
> ask for. Keep on seeking, and you will find. Keep
> on knocking, and the door will be opened to you.

And that is exactly what happened. I kept asking and did not doubt that it could be done for me. But how is it that a young man with no biblical knowledge at all could know that God would eventually answer him? That was either intuitively discerned or God had chosen him to be used as a vessel to hold good things that humanity hopes to rejoice in hearing. For Paul the apostle said in Romans 9:22–24:

> What if God, intending to show His wrath and
> make His power known, bore with great patience
> the vessels of His wrath, prepared for destruction?
> What if He did this to make the riches of His

glory known to the vessels of His mercy, whom
He prepared in advance for glory—including us,
whom He has called not only from the Jews, but
also from the Gentiles?

Christianity is not a religion; it is a relationship that God wants us to have with him, with nothing in between. When I came to the realization that my good works were actually creating a division between myself and a visit to heaven, I destroyed them. As it says in Isaiah 64:6 in the AMPC:

> For we have all become like one who is unclean
> [ceremonially, like a leper], and all our righteous-
> ness (our best deeds of rightness and justice) is
> like filthy rags or a polluted garment; we all fade
> like a leaf, and our iniquities, like the wind, take
> us away [far from God's favor, hurrying us toward
> destruction].

Would you accept filthy rags from someone who has leprosy? So in shattering my good works, I had in effect thrown the filthy rags between myself and God into an incinerator. There was now a clean space between us. But that was still not the deciding factor. When I was moved to call upon the power of Jesus's name, then God responded with an angry "Be you still!"

But before that, there was a loud bang like a thunderclap. What was that all about? Only after reading different Bibles many times over was the answer revealed to me in Ezekiel 21:17:

> I will also clap My hands together, and I will
> appease My wrath; I, the Lord, have spoken.

The loud *bang* sound was God appeasing his anger against me, for I had finally asked in Jesus's name. Then I was granted five minutes in heaven. That *boom* was a lot of God's anger to be released all at once.

What Christ did for us on the cross is to be the final sacrifice God found acceptable because of Yeshua's complete perfection. No good works can come between yourself and Christ's ultimate sacrifice.

Look at Noah and the rainbow, Abraham and the stars, and Jesus's example of the birds and the lilies. Much if not all the way God communicates through nature is nonverbal. It goes straight to your heart as his work: a sunset, a budding leaf, and a shooting star. That is how all mankind can be judged for unbelief, by the appreciation of nature. But hard-hearted rebellion is the biggest problem. I have had it too, and you feel proud while your heart becomes hard as steel.

The way I first learned how deep and powerful God's love for us is, was when I was told by the fellowship to send all our love to God as a gift, every bit of it: "Just send all of it to him, and trust him with it."

So I took all the love from all the memories I treasured most and bundled the love into an ethereal package to send as a soul call to God. When I launched it to him (*on the other side of the universe*, I thought), I felt like I had been gutted of everything that was important to me and I was alone in a vast and empty world. I felt like I had been scraped from the inside of all that was ever important to me.

Then, from the same trajectory that I had launched the gift of love, a powerful love came into me that was a hundred times more powerful than all the love I was able to send to him. The love of God was so overpowering that it brought me to tears. So even though I was having nothing to do with the Bible and knew Jesus's name only, *Adonai* responded to the sacrifice of all my love.

I gave all my love to God, and he returned a love to me that was at least ten times greater than all I could send to him. When Balaam talks about Yahweh, it is the special name by which God had made himself known to his people directly. Balaam's ancestors probably had learned about the living God from Abraham, and he had passed it onto their children.

Six hundred years after Abraham, Balaam also knew the living God. Balaam had to have known that God had promised Abraham to bless these people. For in Genesis 12:3, God said, "I will bless those who bless you, and he who dishonors you I will curse."

I was in a similar situation, as *even after* my five minutes in heaven, I still did not want to open the Bible or acknowledge Jesus as Lord. I had begun to fear God and recognize that he knows all things. And God has a plan for us all and knows our wants and needs before even asking him. Even some of his greatest servants who served God in his temple did not know him intimately right off the bat. First Samuel 3:7 says:

> Now Samuel did not yet know the Lord: The
> word of the Lord had not yet been revealed to
> him.

I was in a similar situation, but my lack of knowledge was because of an unwillingness to read the Word of God and accept his Son as King over all creation. I did not even know about Israel or the Jews because it had not been taught in public schools. But I still recall my mother saying to my sisters and I, "Don't you want to join a church?"

We all shook our heads and said, "No."

I believe my reluctance was due to peer pressure. Although I recall at age twelve, I had an argument with my best friend's mother while she was driving us in her Volkswagen Super Beetle to her LDS church. She was saying that Jesus was the Son of God. She finally said, "Well, at least he existed."

"No, he did not!" I said. I almost got thrown out of the car.

Jesus had not been mentioned in public school at all, so as far as I knew, he did not exist. To go back even farther to another such battle that I was a secret witness to would be to review what was a peaceful Saturday afternoon when I was ten.

I was lying on my bed in the upstairs bedroom and reading an *Adventures of Tintin* picture book when I heard the ring of the doorbell. I walked down to the stairwell and stopped on the landing to look down and see that my eldest sister opened the door and two elderly ladies introduced themselves to her.

"Hello, I am Mrs. Stravinsky, and this is Mrs. Yamaguchi, and she is a Christian convert."

I went back up the stairs and to my book until I heard a loud argument start up at the front door. I looked around the corner of the landing to see that my sister was holding the front door wide open with her left hand.

"What, you believe some 'god' waved a magic wand, and *poof* there was the universe? Ha!" She then slammed the door in their faces so hard that the whole house shook.

The human mind remembers 50 percent of yesterday and 25 percent of the day before and diminishes from there until it whittles down to 1 percent or less, unless a particular memory is associated with a specific feeling, situation, or traumatic event. Memory association can also be used as a tool for recollection. Like when I recalled the following Monday at school, my class was standing outside waiting for the teacher to arrive and open the door to our fourth-grade classroom.

"Look at the beautiful sky and clouds and stars that God made," said Hugh, looking up. "Isn't he amazing with all that he has created?"

I felt just as incensed as my sister had just two days earlier and said, "What, you believe that some 'god' waved a magic wand, and *poof* there was the universe? Ha!"

But Hugh turned around and looked at me with such shock that I felt ashamed. Then, I promised myself that I would never do that again—to anybody.

In 1 Samuel 3:9–10, God spoke through the darkness to Samuel as a boy, "Samuel, Samuel!"

Samuel didn't know who was calling him and asked the high priest, Eli, what he wanted. Eli knew it was from God, so Eli said to Samuel, "Go and lie down, and if he calls you, say, 'Speak, Lord, for your servant is listening.'"

The next time the Lord called, Samuel replied, "Speak, Lord, for your servant is listening."

Then the Lord said to Samuel, "I am going to do a shocking thing in Israel. I am going to do all of the dreadful things I warned Eli about. I have continually threatened him and his entire family with punishment because his sons are blaspheming God, and he doesn't stop them. So I have vowed that the sins of Eli and of his sons shall never be forgiven by sacrifices and offerings."

What can we learn about the Lord from this account?

- God is calling the people to follow him, even when we are in deep deception. He can breach it when we step forward in faith, calling upon the power of the name of Jesus.
- God calls us, even when we aren't looking for him. When I said, "God, you're there!", I was just declaring my faith in him, and then I was going to look for a church to join. I was going to join the religious club, but that was not God's plan for me. I had no idea that he would open a portal between the third heaven and earth to say "Yes, I AM!" to my face.
- God opens our heart and mind so that we can hear and receive him and plug into him and receive his provision.

The good works of sacrifices and offerings were not going to stop the coming punishment of death, because of unending rebellion. I have often had a rebellious attitude, but when God corrected me, I repented. The bravest thing a person can do is ask God for judgment. I have done this, and I am not yet ready to reveal what God said to me.

There is a veil of darkness that does not allow truth to enter, and the truth becomes distorted by the veil. Since the world is spiraling down into deep darkness, it will seem like God is becoming more and more distant. But if you hear God call your name from the darkness, be like Samuel and say, "Speak, Lord Jesus, for your servant is listening." He can reach out at any instant and give you confirmation that he is always present. He may also give you a correction for which you are not prepared. You must repent immediately.

There was a time when I was out of work for a while, and things were not looking good. The numbers were looking more and more bleak as time went on. I was grumbling more and more but continued to read the Bible and attend the Baptist church I was going to at the time. One afternoon, I was heading down the stairs to my basement bedroom to pray when a thought occurred to me. I had been reading from Job where God said to him, "Of course you made the world, because you're so old!" Then I concluded that since God could get sarcastic with Job, then I could get sarcastic with God.

So I went down into my prayer room, which was an old coal room that I had converted into a walk-in closet. As I knelt down in front of the bookcase facing east, I thought about what I was going to say in prayer. "Oh, thank you, Lord God, for this wonderful job," I said sarcastically. "Oh, the money is just rolling in!"

A black hole opened in my ceiling, and God yelled, "Don't you ever do that again!"

Terrified of his sudden anger for a few moments, I then hung my head in shame and said, "Yes, Lord." Then the hole closed up and was gone.

That following Sunday morning, I went for a walk with the Baptist preacher through a grove of newly planted trees and told him what had happened. He just smiled and said, "God will not be mocked."

God was so angry with me that time that he was within a half inch of destroying me on the spot. I wondered why he didn't and looked it up in the Bible. The Holy Spirit led me to a passage:

> They disciplined us for a little while as they thought best, but God disciplines us for our good in order that we may share His holiness. (Hebrews 12:10)

And Hebrews 12:6 says:

> For the Lord disciplines the one He loves, and He chastises every son He receives.

Even before that day when I said, "God, you're there," he has been giving me experiences that led me to the Bible where it can be confirmed that his word is true.

When I was an atheist of nineteen years old and about to join the US military, God had me visit a rich man in hell through my second out-of-body experience. I had idolized that person though he died to the world decades before. That was his first death. All these years later, I can now confirm it from his word in Luke 16:

> The time came when the beggar died and the angels carried him to Abraham's side. The rich man also died and was buried. In Hades, where he was in torment, he looked up and saw Abraham far away, with Lazarus by his side. So he called to him, "Father Abraham, have pity on me and send Lazarus to dip the tip of his finger in water and cool my tongue, because I am in agony in this fire."

The rich man was in hell and still telling others what to do, just as the man in hell did to me just before I joined the Air Force. He gave me a series of orders though he knew he was in hell because he wanted me to become a sort of diplomat to the living world for him. This is rebellious belligerence at its lowest and most persistent level, which is yet another reason why certain rich types will not be going to heaven.

This also makes the confirmation that it was not just a parable that Jesus told, but he is letting us know that there are people in hell currently experiencing their second death—a lot of them. This is because not only would they not repent in life, but they would lock the doors of hell behind them so that they could continue in their rebellion against God to the very last second before all of creation is destroyed. Physical death and pain will be abolished in heaven, but the second death pain will last eternally: born once, die twice, once to the world and then be destroyed on judgment day; born again, die once, and then stay in heaven.

My pre-rapture experience was given to me as a gift of grace by God so that I could pass it on to you and give you hope for what glorious things await you in heaven and to let you know that the rapture is for real, like when Noah closed the door of the ark during the rain and all the unbelievers were outside and drowning. God sealed the door of the ark shut, effectively nailing all the outside rebels into their coffins. But in the next judgment, the world will be blasted with fire.

As it says in 2 Peter 3:

> But by the same word the heavens and earth that now exist are stored up for fire, being kept until the day of judgment and destruction of the ungodly.

So why was I raptured up to heaven as if I were on a cross? Because we have all fallen short of God's mark of excellence and we all deserve to be on that cross. But as Jesus died on that cross for us as a perfect substitute, we are yanked up to heaven by his grace on a symbolic cross with all sins paid for by him. Heaven is not an all-inclusive theme park to which you pay an entrance fee; it is a strictly exclusive kingdom, which no one can enter, except by accepting Jesus as Lord, Master, Savior, and God, with an open mind for whatever God has in mind for you.

*****

When I was in middle school, I had a very interesting history teacher. He actually had quite a sense of humor. He told us in class that when he and his wife went to London, they were standing across the street from the tower that holds the Big Ben bell and the clock that strikes it. But the clock was not working that day. "See," he said to his wife, "you have a face that could stop a clock." She glared at him.

Then he went on to tell us about how we were on the brink of a nuclear holocaust. "Can you imagine some day in the future when archeologists are digging around in this area? They'll pull out from the ground half a burnt desk or half a burnt book." It was then I looked out the window of the bungalow classroom I was in and thought about how I hoped to be the last one to see that mushroom cloud go off in the distance. I was actually hoping for it. Such was the mind of an ungodly thirteen-year-old.

Then when I was fifteen, and I decided that I had to visit my father. My mother warned me that he was a horribly narcissistic person, but a child has to make a connection with a biological parent, regardless of the dangers and loss of security.

When I made it to the airport in Raleigh, North Carolina, we greeted each other with a hug, and there was a brief joy. But on the long, dark drive through the pine forests of Raleigh, there was a cold silence between us. And then I knew there was already a lack of communication. The rest of the stay with him was how he worked and drank and mocked God. I didn't understand at the time that mocking makes a failure to communicate worse.

One time, while we were watching a *Star Trek* rerun, I finally worked up the courage to ask him that all-important question. "Dad, what is the meaning of life?"

He looked at me with a mean grin and said, "Life is a big sh——t sandwich, and every day is just another bite."

My worst fears were confirmed by that one reply. After six months of me trying to connect again and again, I realized it was hopeless and returned to California. Then came the despair of not having a father and knowing you are different from the others. Sad and depressed, I sat on a stool in graphic arts class and looked at a piece of linoleum upon which I was supposed to carve a design. But nothing came to mind, nothing at all.

Then from across the room, a boy cried out, "Hey, you want to play a game?" I looked around. *What? Who? Me? Was someone actually talking to me?*

"If you don't get over here, we'll get someone else," he quipped.

I ran over to where four boys were gathered around him. "What do I do?" I said four times.

David said, "The game is called Dungeons and Dragons," he replied. "We need a fourth player to cast spells, so you'll be a magic-user/cleric."

My depression suddenly changed to extreme happiness and excitement, from the promise of adventure with friends. Indeed, I made more friends and went on a great many medieval campaigns until I became a dungeon master myself.

One of my friends was a Christian, Willie. He was the funniest friend a teenager could have, and one time, he confided an interesting story to me. "I was in the backyard of my house, and I lit a Styrofoam cup on fire. I started turning around, and the flaming cup became a spaceship on fire, and from the flaming dribbles, I heard people screaming as they fell off the spaceship." I was so fascinated by this display of creative intelligence that I told my best friend, Mark, the next day.

Mark just laughed and said, "He was high as a kite. He smokes pot, you know."

No, I did not know. Here I was, a completely law-abiding atheist, and he was a Christian breaking the law. I was perplexed and realized that smoking pot was wrong because it adversely affected the mind.

So what does God say about drugs and alcohol?

I myself did not want anything to do with drugs or alcohol, as I saw many times what it does to the human mind and body, purely from a secular standpoint. God wants us all to be of clear mind and able body at all times, to be able to deliver edifying messages when called upon. God did destroy two men in the wilderness when they were drunk with strong drink.

Nadab and Abihu were going to be great priests for the people. The holy God of Israel had personally set them apart to serve as priests. They were adorned in new robes and sashes, and the turbans on their heads held a golden plate that said, "HOLY to the LORD." They were set apart to serve God, but not for long. The opening verses of Leviticus 10 read:

> Now Nadab and Abihu, the sons of Aaron, each
> took his censer and put fire in it and laid incense
> on it and offered unauthorized fire before the
> LORD, which He had not commanded them.

> And fire came out from before the LORD and
> consumed them, and they died before the LORD.

So their weird tiny fire from coals on a shovel was met with a flamethrower from God, and they were roasted on the spot. The whole gathering of thousands were shocked and terrified. Then their scorched bodies in burnt robes were tossed into the village dump. They were burnt up in dishonor before God. That's one of the reasons why I do not think that the faithful should be cremated.

Ashes are a biblical symbol of mourning and self-abasement. Even so, all those who are believers and have been cremated, whether by accident, war, or final wishes, will be raised in the next resurrection. The Bible teaches that there will be not just one resurrection but a series of resurrections, some to eternal life in heaven and some to the second death as revealed in Daniel 12:2 and John 5:28–29. The first great resurrection has already happened; it was the resurrection of Jesus Christ and a great number of the dead at the same time. This is well-documented in each of the four Gospels just after Christ's death on the cross.

So why did those two of Aaron's decide to get loose and disobey the Lord by creating their own brand of funky fire and offering it to God? Consider this next part of Leviticus 10:

> And the Lord spoke to Aaron saying, "Drink *no
> wine* or *strong drink*, you or your sons with you,
> when you go into the tent of meeting, *lest you die*."

So the sons of Aaron must have been drinking wine or strong drink to summon the courage (or have enough foolishness) to offer God something he did not command. They probably poured some of the strong drink on the coals, which would make the fire turn from red to blue. Fortunately for me, and us all, we live in the age of grace because I have put God to the test a number of times and come within an inch of his ultimate wrath. Some of those moments will be captured in this book.

Marijuana and other such recreational drugs are not to be used either. For those types of drugs or *pharmakeia* will be used worldwide to cause confusion and mislead the nations. For in the use of such drugs and wide distribution thereof, the world will be easily deceived.

Also in the New Testament, in 1 Peter, Paul said, "Be sober-minded, be watchful. Your adversary the devil prowls about like a roaring lion." So don't take the bait.

Paul the apostle also said that Satan dresses as an angel of light. This I can confirm firsthand, as I was praising God in my pitch-black basement room, and I felt something evil was coming up behind me and looked over my left shoulder. A ghostly apparition came through the cement wall behind me, like a man in a white robe and cowl, glowing in the likeness of moonlight, with a scepter in his right hand.

I was confused as to what I was seeing and thought, *What in the world is that?* Then the Holy Spirit came down quickly unto me like a silken parachute with a cowl and no face. And then I saw that the other apparition with the scepter was Satan himself coming to accuse me before God.

This is not the full story by any means, just the gist of it to let you know that we are not safe on this earth from Satan *unless* God has a *hedge of protection* around you and the Holy Spirit has enveloped you from your faith in Jesus and you have access to the Holy Spirit to open your eyes to deception and confusion. Pray every day for God to keep a hedge of protection around you and those you love.

As it says in Job (Iyov) 1:6 in the CJB:

> It happened one day that the sons of God came to serve Adonai, and among them came the Adversary. Adonai asked the Adversary, "Where are you coming from?" The Adversary answered Adonai, "From roaming *through the earth*, wandering here and there."

Satan had come *through* the earth behind me, as I was in my old basement coal cellar that I had converted into a walk-in closet. Behind the cement wall he had come through was dirt, or *earth*.

And Job 9 says:

> The Adversary answered Adonai, "Is it for nothing
> that Iyov fears God? You've put a *protective hedge*
> around him, his house and everything he has."

That was Satan's way of getting to a man who feared God and did what he could to appease God. After I feared God and was given my five minutes in heaven, Satan has been finding ways to stop me from telling the world of the hope in what God has to offer.

Satan the dishonest skeptic

Ever since the talking serpent in the Garden of Eden convinced Eve to eat from the tree of good and evil, we have been on the outside of paradise and enduring life on a world controlled by Satan. This will not always be the case, but for now, we have to be ready for anything.

Satan caused doubt by taking what is true and twisting it just enough to make it into a lie. As Paul the apostle said, "A half-truth is a whole lie."

Other tactics are to change the subject of the argument during the course of conversation when the debate is getting too close to disclosure of the truth.

A dishonest skeptic will also shift the subject of the argument to defend his false position and hide it. You have to be fast and catch them at this, practice makes perfect, and there are lots of YouTube videos on apologetics. Pick one that works for you.

They are often bullies, trying to yell and shut you down from your high position of revealing the truth. They want to pull you down to their level so they can finish you off. They will also try to ridicule and tease you into submission, so fight back by pointing out their obvious faults in a way that will make the audience laugh.

Honest doubters are like *doubting Thomas*, who said, "Except I shall see in his hands the print of the nails, and put my finger into the print of the nails, and thrust my hand into his side, I will not believe." I am much the same way. The proof is not just *in* the pudding but *in the tasting* of the pudding. That is how you know it is good and right.

As it says in Psalm 34:8:

> Taste, and see that ADONAI is good. How
> blessed are those who take refuge in him!

Of the entire Jewish council, Nicodemus was the only rabbi to be an honest doubter. He said to Jesus in secret, "Rabbi, we know that thou art a teacher come from God, for no man can do these miracles that thou doest—except God be with him."

So if you are still skeptical, it is best to enjoy a paradigm shift and be like doubting Thomas. Stay open-minded, and let the golden rays of truth shine down into the murky waters of this world to reveal the hidden realities, for I have to align myself with the apostle Paul, Thomas, and Nicodemus to say that all things have to prove themselves true. And when they do, embrace them as fact and jettison the disproven.

Look at what Jesus said in Luke 17:33:

> Those who try to gain their own life will lose it; but
> those who lose their life for my sake will gain it.

So the life that is now your physical life as it is and your refusal to renounce Jesus will gain the life that is to come in heaven. Your everlasting OOB life is intimately connected to the same personality you have now. These are two points in time of the same eternal life. You who are now on earth will be released to the glorified body in heaven.

Here is a perfect example of how my physical body and eternal life were preserved by refusing to renounce Jesus. Once again, in the basement bedroom of my haunted house on Ellis Avenue in Boise, I awoke with my eyes closed, and I was aware that a hand was in my chest and squeezing my heart. Automatically, I said, "Jesus is my Lord and Master." The hand squeezed my heart until it started hurting, and then I said, "Jesus is my Lord, Master, and Savior and my God." The hand squeezed my heart so hard, I thought it was going to burst, and I said, "Jesus is my Lord, my Master, my Savior, and my God, and I will never renounce him!"

Then, my eyes flew open, and I saw that a dark shadow was hovering directly above me. It was looking at me straight in the eyes. I looked down and saw that it was slowly pulling its hand out of my chest. Then, it flew in a half circle over my bed and went straight through a cement wall. I said, "Yeah, you better get outta here."

C. S. Lewis was called by God to minister, but he didn't want to. In his book *Surprised by Joy*, he revealed that he knew God much better than the clergy. One thing he said that really opened my eyes was, "Hymns were (and are) extremely disagreeable to me."

Most songs in any hymnal are not biblical or at least some of the passages. Some songs mock God like "Happy Angel Band." As you know, there is no such thing as I have revealed to you. Only the most stuck in the mud of human tradition church would sing it. And the song "Old Time Religion" mocks the church.

Perhaps he let the old man in his atheist pride get the better of him, which is very easy to do, as when I wrote that novel that God did not want me to write, I let the old man in me take the helm and "just go wild." The old atheist in me took over and pieced together imaginations from years ago and turned them into an epic novel of the most unbiblical fashion, but not without cost, as the old man in me took over my personal and thought life as well, like in the book *The Metamorphosis* by Franz Kafka. That is why the apostle Paul warns us not to allow the old man or pre-salvation thought process to take over. If you give him an inch, he'll take a yard of your life away.

*****

Despite my reading the *Necronomicon*, God's plan for me was not thwarted. But the day after I had finished reading it, I was given a warning, like the witch of Endor upon seeing Samuel come up from the depths of the earth.

The day after I finished reading the *Necronomicon*, I was watching MTV in my Air Force dorm room. A vision of my father in hell appeared before me. When he stepped through the smoke toward me, he wore no clothes. But there was a vapor drifting around his waist that prevented me from seeing him naked. He glared at me with his jaw clenched for a few moments and then turned around and went back into hell.

I was amazed by the vision and knew full well that it was indeed my father and was looking at me from his position in hell. As an honest, doubting atheist, I could not dismiss the experience. So I stored it away to find the answer later.

I also realized that while my father glared at me in anger, he did not warn of the path to hell I was on. His jaw was clenched, and his glare said it all: *I'll see you in hell.* That was the message he was conveying to me, even though he was the one who had me write out the US Constitution in full while he was in the hospital with pneumonia. He loved his country and himself, but mocked God.

As it says in Luke 23:28:

> There will be weeping and gnashing of teeth, for
> you will see Abraham, Isaac, Jacob, and all the
> prophets in the Kingdom of God, but you will
> be thrown out.

At least the rich man in hell Jesus spoke of asked Abraham to warn his brothers of the path to hell they were on. And as I learned in my psychology classes, 80 percent of human communication is nonverbal.

When my dad last clenched his jaw at me, he revealed a true hatred of me, completely undeserved because I tried to find common ground—but there was none to be had. Also, those who are weeping in hell will do so because they have finally realized the world religions have deceived them, like me, when I wept after Christ put his hand on me and I realized I had been deceived by the world for eighteen years.

Jesus said it best in Matthew 24:30:

> And then shall appear the sign of the Son of man
> in heaven: and then shall all the tribes of the
> earth mourn, and they shall see the Son of man
> coming in the clouds of heaven with power and
> great glory.

So this is yet another cross for me to bear, to tell all people the good news that they can get a free pass into heaven through complete faith in Jesus alone.

CHAPTER 4
Are Out-of-Body Experiences from God?

Out-of-body experiences occur when the soul (your eternal conscious awareness) separates from your physical body even for only a few minutes. It often happens when clinical death and then resuscitation occur, and the patient recalls all the events that happened while they were clinically dead. That would be classified as a near-death experience or NDE.

My first OOB (out-of-body) experience was at the age of twelve. I had just laid down on my bed in the upstairs bedroom to go to sleep when the whole bed suddenly fell through the floor and down to the living room below. The head of the bed slammed onto the living room floor first, and then the end of the bed hit the floor second. Then I sat up in bed, horrified! But I looked around and realized I was still in my own bedroom upstairs.

So what happened? I had many dreams before, and none of them ever gave a dramatic physical feeling of falling through the floor. It was the first real OOB experience for me. It was not until I joined a fellowship that I was actually able to control the OOB experience through yoga and get to do things outside the physical body. Those are things of which I will not talk about in this book, as certain events transpired that are not in the Bible so far as I have found. But there are parts in the Bible unto which I can say with absolute certainty that are OOB experiences that God had ordained.

Through my failed experiments as an atheist to get an OOB experience through astral projection, I learned that something was missing. But what?

It was not until after my declaration that God was there and I feared God. Two weeks later, I asked him for five minutes in heaven, and he gave me my first OOB experience through rapture so that I could actually be there. Paul the apostle said that he was not sure whether his heaven experience was in the body or out of the body.

His OOB experience may have happened after the Jewish leaders that came from Antioch and Iconium persuaded the crowds to stone Paul to death and drag him out of the city. While Paul was in heaven, he *heard* things that he said were not supernaturally legal for a person to speak about in this world.

In 2 Corinthians 12, Paul wrote:

> I know a man in Christ about 14 years ago (whether he was in the body I cannot tell, or whether he was out of the body I cannot tell, God knows) who was taken up into the third Heaven. And I know the same man (whether in the body or out of the body I do not know, God knows) He was taken up into Paradise and heard words not to be spoken, which no man can utter.

While I was in heaven, I did not hear anything, and I believe it was because as Paul said, "Faith comes by hearing and hearing through the word of Christ." I did not have any faith in the Word of Christ at the time, and so I had no spiritual hearing while I was in heaven.

It could also be that as Paul said *he heard words that were not lawfully to be spoken.* And since I did not know at the time what words you hear in heaven are not to be repeated on earth, perhaps that is why I could not hear them being spoken while I was there. For instance, I could not hear what the people in the white robes were shouting.

Also, there was no one to greet me in heaven, for the people in the white robes did not see me as they were walking to the left and right in delight and occasionally stopping to praise God, Jesus, and the Holy Spirit. All persons appeared to be in their late twenties to early thirties. I did see one woman with shoulder-length black hair some sixty feet away, walking to the right in the same way as the others. She may have been my grandmother who had that style of hair in her twenties. She was a Christian who died years before my five minutes in heaven, and she last knew me as a teenage atheist. Perhaps due to distance and preoccupation, she did not notice me, and I did not recognize her. But I think it was more likely that it was by God's design that she did not greet me because I only used the power of Jesus's name to beg for a visit to heaven and my time was short.

So by God's grace and mercy, I was there in heaven for five minutes because God's list of determining factors had been completed for your benefit and mine. None of those factors included good works because I had destroyed them all before God. For God said to Moses, "I will show mercy to anyone I choose, and I will show compassion to anyone I choose."

*****

Now, God gave OOB power to Elisha when Israel was getting ambushed by their enemies. This was put to a stop by God when he allowed Elisha to go in the spirit to spy on the enemy in their king's own private room. As it says in 2 Kings 6:12, "One of his servants said, 'No, my lord, O king; but Elisha, the prophet who is in Israel, tells the king of Israel the words that you speak in your bedroom.'"

So Elisha, while in the spirit, was able to travel to enemy territory undetected and then hear and see everything in the king's own bedroom without them being aware of his presence. To give you a present-day example, a woman I know had a cowboy dancing partner who, unbeknownst to her, was able to travel OOB. This is how she found out.

While lying in her bed, she was awakened at one in the morning by the feeling that someone was looking at her. She looked at the wall in front of her and saw her cowboy friend was sticking halfway through the wall in a semitransparent body. He was looking down at her from the top-left part of the wall. She screamed in horror, and he looked surprised and disappeared into the wall.

So it can happen to anyone at any time. It's best to be prepared by wearing the full armor of God.

I tried to return

It was two weeks after my visit to heaven that I asked God to let me into heaven again, and there was no response. That is when I knew that I would not return until my time on earth was finished, and I would have to continue on my travels across the paths of the world until my time was complete. What I did not know at the time was that I had been thrown out of heaven, like the parable of the man who went to the wedding party improperly dressed.

In Matthew 22:11, God's Word says:

> During the wedding feast, the King noticed a man who was *not* dressed in wedding attire. When asked how he came to be there in street clothes, the man could not reply. So the man was bound, and then eighty-sixed out of the feast area and sent into the outer darkness where there is weeping and gnashing of teeth.

At the end of the parable, Jesus said, "For many are *invited* but few are *chosen*." In comparison, the last moment I was in heaven looking at the Tree of Life and realizing my time was up; the very next second, the head of my spirit-man slammed into the chest of my physical body, and the breath of life came back to my body.

In the parable, the wedding feast represented heaven, the king was God, the groom was Christ, and the outer darkness was hell.

The reason I was thrown out of heaven was fourfold: my five minutes were up, the wedding feast is still yet to be, I was not saved, and I did not yet believe in God's Word.

The reason I was not thrown into the outer darkness or hell is threefold: God knew that I would eventually be saved by his own Son appearing in my room and putting his hand on me, thereby having to accept the Bible as the epicenter of truth; God does not want to have to send any human to hell; that is an unlivable place designed to hold Satan and his rebel angels. He wants to save you so that the silver cord will pull you up to heaven and not down to hell.

We see those who are living as if we are all marching in a formation. We see those who are in front and behind and to the left and right as those who are alive. God is high above us and sees where we are going in the passages of time. He sees those who have died that are behind us and those who are ahead of us that have yet to be born. He sees them all at the same time because he is omnipotent and omnipresent. He can be at any and all places at any time. That is how Christ came to my room and physically put his right hand on my right shoulder.

Exactly what Christ said in Luke 12:51, I find most precisely put in The Message Bible. He said that he did not come to make everything all nice and peaceful. He came to *disrupt and confront*. When he put his right hand on my shoulder, he confronted me on my worldly belief system and then disrupted it to its very foundation.

When Jesus held me captive for those two minutes and spoke those words into my right ear canal, I no longer had a choice to reject him. As he said in John 10:27–28, "My sheep hear my voice, I know them and they follow me." Christ has his own version of the *Quantum Leap* and keeps his own body.

God is also omnipotent and has unlimited power and authority over everything created. He is also omniscient and knows all things and all technologies at all times. Finally, he also has omnibenevolence as Adonai is always perfectly good. In Mark 10:18, Jesus said, "Why do you call me good? No one is good—but God alone."

*****

Years later, I came to question whether or not certain OOB experiences were from God, and so in my basement bedroom at my house in the north end of Boise, Idaho, I prayed, "Oh, Adonai, if out-of-body experiences are of your intent and making, please give one to me. And let me know that it is in your Word with a confirmation."

The first night after that prayer, I slept soundly, and there wasn't even a single dream—I slept in darkness. But the next night, I woke up at about one in the morning, and the basement bedroom was dark and quiet. Something strange in the air had awakened me, and I was aware that there was a presence.

Suddenly, a silver cord rose up from the left side of my stomach like a tentacle, and it wrapped around the base of my spine just above my pelvis. Then it yanked me down through the bed and through the cement floor. I was being pulled backward through the earth as if all the dirt and underground boulders flying past me were made of warm water.

I was screaming as I was being pulled backward down to the center of the earth, until I popped out the other side of the world. Then I looked around and could see the sun and surrounding territory—it was about two o'clock in the afternoon. There was a vast land of tall yellow grass and low flat-topped trees, and then I realized I was hovering twenty feet above the plains of the Serengeti in broad daylight.

Looking down, I saw a small herd of about fourteen Thomson's gazelles quietly eating grass. All at once, they stopped eating the grass and slowly looked up toward me. When they saw me hovering there in my robe, they all became terrified and scattered in all directions. I was pulled back to my own home in Boise, Idaho, and it was still dark. I was in the air and circling around a strange stained glass lamp that was hanging from the ceiling. I was praising God with joy while circling around it.

After that harrowing adventure God had given me, I looked up the word *silver cord* in the Bible for my confirmation. The answer I was given was in Ecclesiastes 12:6: At death, the spirit will be pulled back from earth to heaven by the silver cord:

> Remember Adonai, before the silver cord is sev-
> ered, and the golden bowl is broken; before the
> pitcher (your body) is shattered at the spring, and
> the (potter's) wheel is broken at the well (of life).

Trajectory of the silver cord

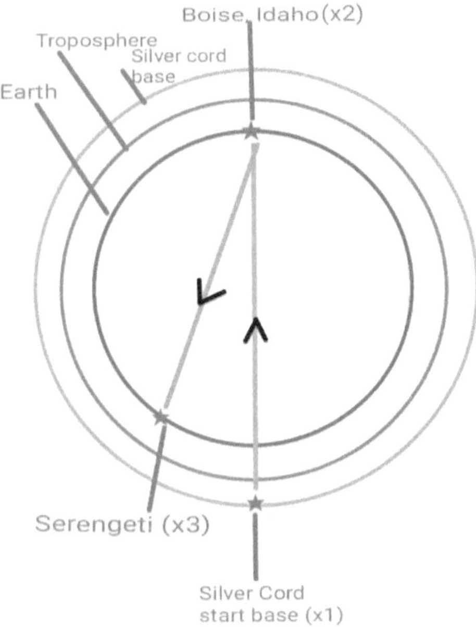

So it is now proven that the silver cord is like a fisherman's line that pulls you up into heaven from your earthly body. That is how we will meet Christ in the clouds as it is stated in 1 Thessalonians 4:17:

> After that, we who are still alive and are left will
> be caught up together with them in the clouds to
> meet the Lord in the air. And so we will be with
> the Lord forever.

Now the silver cord *did not* pull me *from* the center of the earth and then *push* me out the other side to hover over the plains of the Serengeti. Think about it: the outward layer of this planet is measured by its circumference, and when I was raptured, I was pulled straight up to the cirrus cloud layer or troposphere, which is up to 12 miles above the earth's surface.

Note that heaven is a square, a perfect bunker in which to store God's valuables. That would be us. It is 1,500 miles high, wide, and tall. Since the troposphere is only 11 to 12 miles high, how does that work? Well, you cannot go there physically, only OOB at God's will.

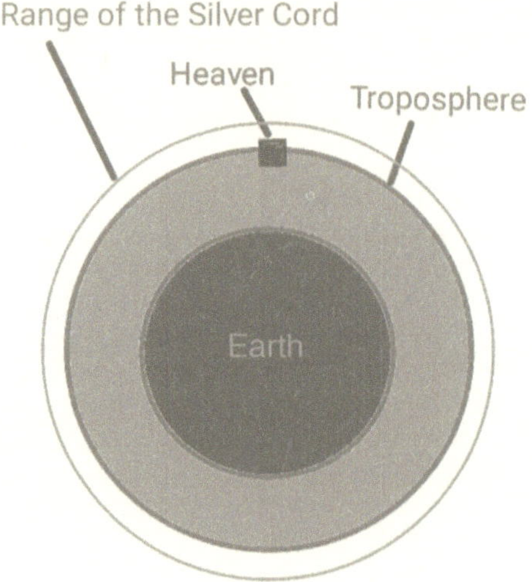

So here is a riddle that bothered me for ages, as it made no sense:

What goes up a chimney down, but not down a chimney up?

This Victorian riddle confused me for a long time. But it made me think: Does the silver cord only go down, or does it also go up?

It is more easily understood by my Uncle Richard who lived in Kampen, The Netherlands.

My Uncle Richard's death

On the night my mother went OOB involuntarily, she was whisked away to the Netherlands to witness her brother Richard's passing. He was a World War II veteran and a Royal Dutch Marine Corp major. Here is what happened in her own words:

> I was walking down the street in Kampen where Richard lived alone. I could feel the cobblestones on my bare feet as I walked down the street to his house. I walked through the front door, which was open, and I saw him in his pajamas standing at the top of the stairs. I shouted, "Richard!" He shouted, "Louiseja!" Then a misty cloud swirled around him and pulled him up. He was gone.
>
> Then I heard a knock on the front door in my own home, and heard my son and daughter talking. Then I knew that Richard had died.

So the *coiled cloudy mist* must have come from the heavenly realm as the silver cord, as it is a supernatural creature. Like God's angels, it has a personality and knows exactly what to do.

So how high up is the silver cord? I have pondered this, and the answer was given to me while I was writing.

When I begged God to give me five minutes in heaven, the silver cord (unseen to me at the time) pulled me up to just one foot above the striated cirrus cloud layer. That was in my spirit body, as my physical body could never survive being pulled straight up at 409 mph to 30,000 feet. This is what the rapture experience is all about. You are pulled upward superfast, you're full of joy, and it's tons of fun.

*****

As it says in Isaiah 40:

> God is enthroned above the circle of the earth; its inhabitants are like grasshoppers.

So it shows in the cutaway image God's throne is in heaven above the circle of the earth. Ninety percent is down through the troposphere, and the pearl gate entrances are at the top of the square jasper walls, not the middle. That is because heaven will be lowered down to earth to replace the old Jerusalem as stated in Revelation 21:2:

> And I John saw the holy city, new Jerusalem,
> coming down from God out of heaven, prepared
> as a bride adorned for her husband.

It is about 1,800 miles down to the Earth's core, and heaven is 1,500 miles in height, so that leaves about 300 miles for heaven proper to protrude from the Earth's crust when it lands. The pearl gates would be at the top. But the problem of the molten iron core at the center of the earth comes into play.

As the New Jerusalem is directly in line with the pearl gates, it is possible that John is saying that *only* the New Jerusalem city *itself* will be lowered *from* heaven proper. In this case, the silver cord could act like a quantum sky crane, lowering the New Jerusalem down onto the old Jerusalem from the bottom of the heavenly bunker. This would require further study.

Instead of thinking like man, we have to think like God. The order of the heavens is not troposphere to the exosphere as the first heaven; the sun, moon, and stars in the second heaven; and then the third heaven is somewhere beyond that. It is as my earth cutaway figure shows. The first heaven is the troposphere, and the second heaven is where the stars and galaxies are located. God is not in the atmosphere or the stellar but in the third heaven. The jasper walled bunker in the troposphere.

So the third heaven is just above the troposphere and below the second heaven. It is the jasper-walled, pearl-gated bunker as mentioned in Revelation 21 and 22. Next is the map of heaven as described in Revelation 22:1–2 in conjunction with what I saw firsthand:

> Then the angel showed me the river of the water
> of life, as clear as crystal, flowing from the throne
> of God and of the Lamb down the middle of the

great street of the city. On each side of the river stood the tree of life, bearing twelve crops of fruit, yielding its fruit every month. And the leaves of the tree are for the healing of the nations.

The next image shows a map of where I was standing when I was positioned in heaven during my five minutes. All the gates are named for the tribes of Israel listed in the order from oldest to youngest: Reuben, Simeon, Levi, Yudah, Dan, Naphtali, Gad, Asher, Issachar, Zebulun, Yoseph, and Benyamin.

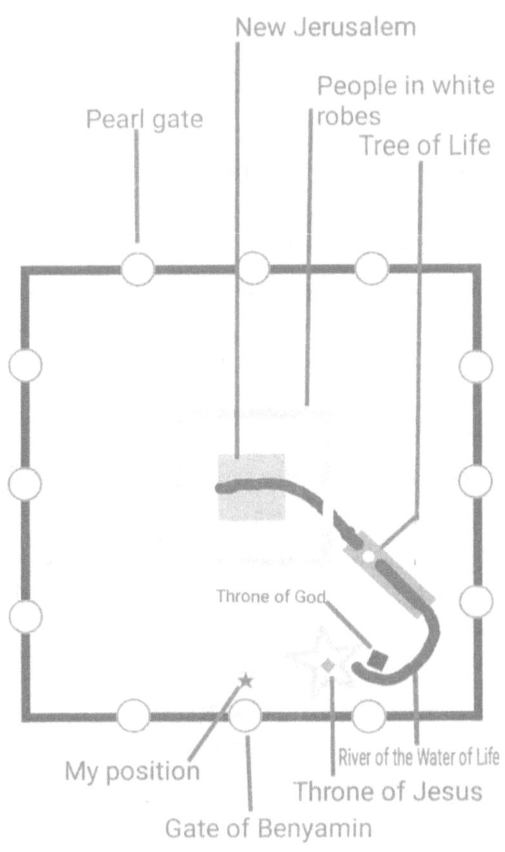

During the rapture, the saved are pulled up in the spirit to the surface of troposphere as Paul said in 1 Thessalonians 4:17:

> Then we who are left still alive will be caught up
> with them in the clouds to meet the Lord in the
> air; and thus we will always be with the Lord.

Referring back to the trajectory of the silver cord image, it had to launch downward from just above the troposphere and through the earth near the southeast coast of Africa and then rocket through the earth to the opposite side of the world and up into my basement bedroom in Boise.

When it rose through the left side of my stomach, it doddled for a few moments (as if savoring the moment) before wrapping around the base of my spine three times and yanking me down into the ground and through to the other side of the earth.

I did not see bedrock on my way down or out the other side, and that is good because according to where hell is far down below, brimstone is mentioned in the Bible and that type of mineral is found in the bedrock layer. *Brimstone*, better known as sulfur, is a biblical term for "God's wrath."

This is a big departure from the average OOB experience of a person, as they never mention the silver cord. Again, it is a thing they did not ask for, as it has only one reference in the Bible. It was a great privilege given to me simply for asking God with a sincere heart and a true hunger for wisdom from his word. I was being real with him, and so he not only let me see the infinite silver cord, but he also let me see how it works.

I used an antipode app to see where the exact opposite side of the earth is from Boise, Idaho. The answer was over the ocean some twenty miles off the coast of South Africa. Now, if the silver cord had grabbed me straight through the earth from the launch point of the troposphere, it would have to do it at an arch-type trajectory. I do recall a few moments while being pulled down; it was done so at a slight curve bending to the right. That was to get me to Tanzania, where the Serengeti plains are located.

Here comes the math

So a Roman soldier walks into a bar. He goes up to the bartender, holds up two fingers, and says, "Five beers please," one of my best nerd jokes; I hope you appreciate the humor. The idea is to break the ice and move into a deeper study, like an ice ship venturing into Antarctica. This requires careful calculating.

The right bend I experienced while going down is like a parabolic equation, or the angle of trajectory of a projectile (with me being the projectile) being pulled down by the silver cord.

A parabola is a symmetrical open curve, formed by the intersection of a circular cone with a plane at a smaller angle than its axis.

The general equation of a parabola is:

$$y = a(x-h)^2 + k \text{ or } x = a(y-k)2+h,$$

where (h,k) denotes the vertex. The standard equation of a regular parabola is y2 = 4ax.

CHAPTER 5
The God of Science

As Albert Einstein once said, "I want to know God's thoughts, the rest are details." So how is it that Einstein came to the understanding that all things are created of energy, as in $E=MC^2$? Basically, his formula says energy is equal to matter going twice the speed of light. So just for a moment, imagine that your new superpower enabled you to throw a baseball faster than the speed of light to the opposite end of the galaxy. It would go something like this: as you wind up for the pitch on a dark starry night and aim for a black hole between the stars, you throw the baseball that would become a long strand of colored light as it reaches the halfway point in the galaxy. By that time, the baseball would be an elongated light spectrum, being red in the back and blue in the front. That is because red light is the slowest and blue light is the fastest, and the other rainbow colors would be in between. Then, as the ball goes faster than the speed of light, its atomic structure breaks down into energy or photons. A photon carries energy but has zero rest mass.

So in the understanding that God can make seemingly inanimate objects turn into living breathing people, so it is that Matthew 3:9–10:

> And don't suppose you can comfort yourselves by saying, "Abraham is our father!" For I tell you that God can raise up for Abraham sons from these stones!

Jesus said, "These stones can become sons of Abraham." How can this be? Well, God created Adam from dust of the earth, a.k.a. minerals. You break the stones down into energy, $E=MC^2$ once again. Humankind is getting very close to this through nanotechnology and quantum mechanics. And all language barriers are being overcome through simple smartphones.

As God said in Genesis 11:6:

> Our Lord God Adonai said, "Behold, they are one people, and they all have the same language. And this is what they began to do, and now nothing which they purpose to do will be impossible for them."

*****

Ecclesiastes was written by the wisest man in the world, King Solomon. God let him be aware of the silver cord also, probably in his younger years. I can't say if he asked God for an OOB experience, but it is possible as this has been happening since Adam and Eve were forced to leave the Garden of Eden.

King Solomon said in Proverbs that a three strong cord is not easily broken. I do recall the silver cord wrapping around my L5 three times before yanking me down. This also means that your spiritual body has a skeleton. How else would you be able to walk around heaven and be seated at the marriage supper of the lamb?

This also means that the silver cord is probably made up of three strands. The curtains of the tabernacle are made of three strands, the curtain ordered by God to be made one of violet and purple, another of scarlet twice-dyed, and fine, twisted linen. However, the silver cord is a translucent blue/white spiritual creature, and in the few seconds of my observing it, I saw only a singular cord.

The veil was the boundary between earth and heaven, but when Jesus died on the cross, the veil was torn open, and through the power of Jesus's name, we have direct access to heaven.

Since OOB has been going on since the fall of mankind, a.k.a. Adam and Eve, it is absolutely impossible for there to be only one silver cord.

People die all the time, and since over 6,000 die per day with saved people being pulled up to heaven and the unsaved being yanked down to hell, the silver cord would *have* to be a creature of quantum mechanics. The silver cord is a noncorporeal thing of such multifaceted speed and complexity that it cannot be defeated, only controlled by God. Think of the movie *The Golem* starring Roddy McDowall.

Quantum mechanics is the branch that deals with the mathematical description of the motion and interaction of subatomic particles, including the quantization of energy, wave-particle duality, the uncertainty principle, and the correspondence principle.

So as the third heaven is up to 10 miles above the earth, the silver cord came down from heaven above the Serengeti and stretched through the entire diameter of the planet, all the way to my basement bedroom of my house in Boise, Idaho. Then, it yanked me downward through my bed and through the earth, to stop just above the herd of Thomson's gazelles on the Serengeti. That means the whole world is 360 degrees and all of heaven surrounds the earth in the same way. So we are pulled upward or downward by the silver cord at God's command wherever we are in the world. Or you can use the circle's diameter: multiply the diameter by π, or 3.1416. The result is the earth's circumference. The silver cord uses quantum tunneling to go through the earth, using the cirrus level of the troposphere as a launch point.

Now, since the silver cord is infinitely more elastic, penetrating, and long-reaching than Wonder Woman's lasso, it can reach *through* the earth from heaven in a linear path and pull you straight up to the cirrus cloud layer, as it did Paul the apostle and many prophets of God. It also did it for me, though the mouth of the whirlwind he sent, which is how it must have done with Elijah, as God sent a whirlwind for him.

Many preachers think that Elijah was caught up into heaven in a fiery chariot. Because they are thinking in a worldly way, they are wrong. Read it carefully for yourself in 2 Kings 2:

> As they were walking along and talking, behold,
> a chariot of fire and horses of fire SEPARATED the
> two of them, and Elijah went up *by a whirlwind*
> into heaven.

The chariot of fire separated the two as chariots do in battle. They charge into a group of soldiers and divide them. As Napoleon once said, "Divide and conquer." God had to separate Elijah from Elisha as it was Elijah's time to return to God. But then, a *whirlwind* took Elijah into heaven. That is God's way of doing things.

This is a good question to ask your pastor: "Did Elijah get caught up to heaven in a fiery chariot?" If he answers yes, then he does not fully know the mind of God, but his (or her) thought process has passed over the original writer's intent. I was given the Elijah treatment sans fiery chariot as I was by myself.

But then, King David was a man after God's own heart and still made mistakes. But his passion was in the right place. Maybe your pastor needs to have the Holy Spirit remove the veil of worldly sight, so that his sight may be fully on spiritual concerns.

I have the opposite problem, in which I know a lot of supernatural and Bible secrets through experience but have a hard time communicating them because I am not a Maverick as in *Top Gun* but more like Dean in *Supernatural*, the TV drama series.

Isaiah despaired

Now Isaiah said in 6:1:

> In the year that King Uzziah died I saw the Lord
> sitting upon a throne, high and lifted up; and
> the train of his robe filled the temple... And the
> foundations of the thresholds shook at the voice

of Him who called, and the house was filled with
smoke. And I said: "Woe is me! For I am lost;
for I am a man of unclean lips, and I dwell in
the midst of a people of unclean lips; for my eyes
have seen the King, the Lord of hosts!"

Here's the breakdown in comparison. Isaiah saw the extent of
his sin from his knowledge and experience with God and compared
it to God's holy perfection. Isaiah despaired, as I did for a moment,
because we knew we could do nothing as humans to fix the errors
of our ways. I realized the futility of good works and destroyed them
before God. After all, what's the use? So we need Christ's holy perfection to bridge the gap over the chasm of troubled water. Indeed,
he has laid himself down for us to cross over to heavenly perfection.

Concerning the rapture

I think that Christ will greet us at the outside walls of heaven
and have us line up at the pearl gates according to our assigned tribe
of Judah. Because of our faith in Christ, we replace the unbelieving dried-up branch that has been pruned. The pruned branches are
cultivated olive branches that grew from the tree. We are wild olive
shoots that are grafted in by faith in Christ and therefore can be
removed and replaced by the natural olive branch that was bred in
Israel, if it finally comes to Christ.

Each of us will be given a white stone with our new name on it,
as we enter into our assigned pearl gate according to the tribe that we
belong to. Our new name will determine which gate we enter, and
then we will join with the people in the white robes where the tribes
can mix and mingle and be.

*****

Now on an interesting side note, the Thomson's gazelles that
saw me in the spirit hovering above them became terrified and fled.
This means that animals can see into the supernatural realm. God's

word confirms this as Balaam's donkey saw the *angel of death*, but Balaam the human didn't until it was almost too late. As it says in Numbers 22:

> But the anger of God burned because he was going. The angel of Adonai stood in the road to oppose him he was riding on his donkey and two of his servants were with him when *the donkey saw the angel of Adonai* standing in the road with his drawn sword in his hand, the donkey turned off the road and went into the field.

The donkey not only saw and knew that the angel was there to kill Balaam, but it did what it could to save his life. So there is a lot more going on in the animal kingdom than what we see on nature documentaries. God had created different creatures to accomplish various tasks and given spiritual awareness to them as well.

God can also use man-made objects to save your life in unexpected ways, like when I prayed a prayer using the *prayer language of the angels* to protect my X3 and me while traveling. Three days later, the X3 did something bizarre that ended up saving my life. No mechanic can figure out why it did what it did at precisely the right time to keep me safe.

Three-dimensional thinking

So to get in the proper mind perspective, a line from Star Trek's *The Wrath of Khan* comes to mind. The starship Enterprise was in a desperate battle with a Klingon battle cruiser controlled by the mega-bully Kahn, as I recall. Then Captain Kirk realized that Kahn was fighting in a linear or line-of-sight mindset. That is called *two-dimensional thinking.* So the captain flew the Enterprise above the Klingon battle cruiser and bombarded Kahn from above, taking him by surprise and causing mega-damage.

So God's thinking and ways of doing things are completely different from the world's way. The world is stuck on no-God (stuck inside the box) thinking. But God's mind is far above the mind of the world, and the bombardment will come during the Great Tribulation. That tragedy is going to be way beyond the flood that drowned the world during Noah's time, as it says in Revelation 16:21:

> And there fell upon men a great hail out of heaven,
> every stone about the weight of a talent…

A talent, if equivalent to a talent of silver, would weigh about 60 pounds. What house or car in this world can withstand the fall of hundreds of 60-pound boulders crashing down on them? Just another reason why we do not want to be a part of this world when the Holy Spirit departs. And I have seen the Holy Spirit on two occasions, and each time it landed on me, it was as gentle as a dove and revealed the truth to me. Though to me, it felt more like a silken sheet gently landed on me. That is to encapsulate the one who has Christ like a cloak with his or her face in the cowl and protect them from deception.

Heaven, we have a problem

To compare our rapture liftoff to heaven with a rocket trajectory, computation to the cirrus cloud layer requires a little math. I love math, and I hope you do too. I did binary-level troubleshooting for eight-layer Internet switch circuit cards during twelve-hour graveyard shifts for my engineering team. Communicating with computer chips in binary makes time fly, as you get lost in a multiverse of *1*s and *0*s. Think of the movie *The Matrix*. So here we go. The required value of maximum height (cirrus cloud layer) is $u2sin2\theta2g$, and the range is $u2sin2\theta g$. *Time of height* is the time when we attain the maximum height of the landing site of the cirrus cloud layer as that is and is given to us by the calculation $t=usin\theta g$.

When we are pulled up by the silver cord, acceleration might not be inhibited by gravity, as the spirit being inside of us is supernatural and does not weigh more than one ounce. Also, our velocity does not change from its initial value, as this is what it felt like on my way up.

This motion is called *vertical projectile motion*. So the velocity of a person in vertical displacement, the moving of something from its original place, caused by the acceleration of gravity is given by:

$Vy = Vy0 - gt$, where:

Vy = Vertical velocity at time t
$Vy0$ = Initial velocity of the person
g = acceleration due to gravity
t = time of flight

From memory, the time of flight was about five seconds from the condo floor to the troposphere level where I saw heaven. And the silver cord was launched from the troposphere at an angle θ with a velocity v. Then the silver cord reached a maximum angle of X and a maximum range of Y. Calculate the value of θ and let X = 10 m/s^2.

Speed of the silver cord

The speed at which the silver cord pulls us up to heaven or down to hell is not difficult to discern, just rudimentary. The tools at which it can be done are simply your hand and your mind.

When I was a kid growing up in San Diego, I went to see a movie about outer space at the Ruben H. Space Fleet planetary theater. At the end of the movie, it showed a cartoon of how to measure the speed and direction of a UFO, should you happen to see one. Aim your fist at the spaceship, and then count the seconds as the UFO moves across the sky: "One-one thousand, two-one thousand, three-one thousand."

That was the only way I could calculate the speed at which the silver cord pulled me downward. I could only use the going-downward recollection as the going-upward rapture experience did not have any milestones through which I could start counting. There was only sky from the moment the mouth of the whirlwind hit me to the moment I was being held aloft by the unseen silver cord just above the cirrus cloud layer.

Through memory and visualization, I recalled how fast the underground boulders went past me as I was being pulled down and counted the seconds. One went over my right shoulder that was the size of a bus, and that is the one I use as a marker. This is the answer: I was being pulled down at about 200 yards per second or 409 miles per hour.

So you can think of all those hundreds of thousands who died at the same time in major earthquakes, wars, and the eruption of Mount Vesuvius at Pompeii just to name a few. The silver cord must be an infinitely multifaceted octopus-like creature just above heaven at the cirrus cloud layer with moveable bases that can quantum-create as many tentacles as it needs to get the job done, 360 degrees around the entire globe. And it does not rest, it is active 24/7.

How does the silver cord discern between good and evil?

The silver cord knows the difference between the saved and unsaved as surely as God knows the minds of us all. As it says in Genesis 6 during the days of Noah before the flood of judgment, "The Lord saw that the wickedness of man was great in the earth, and that every *intention of the thoughts of his heart* was only evil *continually.*"

One thousand six hundred years had passed since Adam and Eve, and as the earth's population grew exponentially, evil also mushroomed and spread throughout all of Pangea. Violence in the mind causes anxiety, heart palpitations, sleeplessness, and hatred until it is dismissed or fulfilled. It cannot be managed, and the only real solution is to dismiss it.

In the movie *The Death of Stalin*, the Supreme Soviet was having a heart attack in his office, and his two bodyguards outside were obeying orders to not disturb him, despite them hearing him hit the floor with a *thud.* His day had come, and the silver cord came up through the floor of his office and grabbed his spirit-man by the

L5 of the lumbar in his spinal column and yanked him down to his designated little holding cell in hell.

God knew the name of every person on Stalin's hit list, and finally, the cries of the lives he destroyed came to reach God at his throne. And now, there Stalin sits in his cell locked from the inside to try to keep God out. But God's mercy reaches even there, as he is allowed visitors. This could be at the insistence of Satan on a day of the angels so that Satan can keep personality cult followers in contact with their icons, thus keeping them ready for the day they are to be released during the Tribulation Period.

So yes, as surely as God knows your every passing thought, the same goes for me. I even had the audacity to ask God to judge me, and I did it in a not-so-nice way. It went like this: as I was driving to work one afternoon, I was listening to a preacher on the radio of my 1973 Firebird. "The bravest thing a man can do is ask God to judge him," he said. I was fearful of what the man said and turned off the radio.

While working my night shift duties of a controls technician, I was putting together an industrial chopping machine when an idea came to mind. I looked at the wall of the factory and said, "Lord God, I want you to judge me, right now!" After all, Christ himself had put his hand on me, and I was well versed in several different Bibles plus asked for forgiveness of all sins in Jesus's name.

When I got home in the morning, I went down to my basement bedroom and into the old coal room, closing the door behind me. I knelt before God, and as I started happily praising him, a black hole opened in my ceiling, and God said, "I have these two judgments against you."

Shocked and taken aback, I said, "What are they, Lord?"

"First of all, you cling to your money as if it could save your life."

"Yes, Lord," I said, "I'm working on that."

Then God said angrily, "And I don't like that book you're writing!" I was floored. Nobody knew about the novel I was writing, and I had saved it under a false utility title on the hard drive.

So I symbolically yielded my book over to God by saying, "Then I turn the book over to you, Lord, for I trust you completely."

I heard a faint clap as the Lord released his final bit of anger against me, and then a powerful vision appeared in front of me, revealing an event that happened in circa 400 BC.

A wide screen vision opened two feet in front of me, and I saw a dark night in the desert with a full moon on the upper left. On the bottom left, I saw a blazing bonfire burning, and a long line of men in white robes and turbans standing before the bonfire. All the men had curly black beards as in ancient times, and they all had a bundle tightly wrapped in white linen resting on their forearms. Then the ceremony began, and I was horrified to see what they were doing. Then the Spirit of the Lord came into me and raged against the men, but they continued what they were doing.

So what happened? Why did God still have two judgments against me despite being saved? The answer is that just like taxes, you have to itemize. You cannot just say, "Lord Jesus, forgive me of all my sins, amen." It doesn't work like that. You have to confess on a daily or sin-by-sin schedule, or those sins will be waiting for you on Judgment Day.

You can allow that to happen if Jesus is your Lord, Master, Savior, and God. He is both the Son of man and the Son of God. Know that he died on the cross to have your sins forgiven and the prophecies of the Old Testament fulfilled, and accept the fact that he died and was resurrected on the third day after entombment.

If you do allow your sins to dawdle till Judgment Day and God calls you out on them at the Great White Throne Judgment, then you will have to say that Jesus is your advocate so that they will be forgiven. Then you can be shuffled over to the Bema Throne Judgment and receive rewards instead of the furnace.

The Great White Throne Judgment is where the unrighteous are in line and can only see the shekinah glory of Jesus and nothing else. His glory outshines all created things, including his own throne. Just as I saw in heaven for the first praising of Jesus before his throne, I only saw a brilliant white light. I then spontaneously glorified Adoni, Yeshua, and the Holy Spirit as I was compelled to. The second time I gloried him, my light must have become brighter, more equal to his, as that is when I saw the right arm rest and left rear foot of his Bema throne. His goal is to get you to be as bright as he is by praising Adonai, Yeshua, and the Ruach HaKodesh. This is so that you can see him clearly, as he really is.

*****

The level to which Christ will bring us in the rapture is as it states in 1 Thessalonians 4:17:

> Then we who are alive, who are left, will be
> caught up together with them in the clouds to
> meet the Lord in the air, and so we will always be
> with the Lord.

Christ went down to hell for three days to talk with those who rejected the preaching of Noah. Then he took them to heaven on the third day. The silver cord pulled Jesus and all of them up to heaven, Jesus being resurrected first.

So a question arises: Who controls the silver cord, God or Jesus? I believe it has been delegated to Jesus from Adonai because Jesus said, "I was dead, and behold, now I am alive forevermore, and *I have the keys to death and Hades*." When you are pulled out of your physical body as I was, both for my five minutes in heaven and two minutes over the Serengeti, it will be by the silver cord.

And both times, I was "absent from the body," and one of those two times, I was "present with the Lord." As Paul the apostle said in 2 Corinthians 5:8, "But we are of good courage and *prefer to be absent from the body* and to *be at home with the Lord*."

*****

There's much spoken about the silver cord of human beings, yet much is left to be known about it. Many people think it is left to the secret societies to glean. Its obscurity in the Bible makes it little known to the Christian faith.

The *silver cord* refers to that life- and soul-preserving cord that connects your soul to your physical body. It refers to the conscious thread, passing from the soul to the physical body that connects the physical body to the spirit or astral body and finally to the conscious mind.

Soul (in the body *or* astral plane of second heaven, third heaven, or hell), mind (brain embodiment), and body (physical embodiment), just that simple. The silver cord keeps the human spirit in the body, like a literal lifeline. This is where life stays connected to the body in order to keep you active as you walk about this world, as long as your heart is beating and you are breathing. Remember to thank Jesus for keeping you alive and that the silver cord remains unsevered for your rapture to heaven.

For as surely as the silver cord can be used by Christ to pull you up into heaven at lightning speed, it can also drag you down into hell just as fast. That same silver cord pulled me down to the center of the earth and had me hovering over the Serengeti. It could also have dropped me off in hell and left me there. But it held me over the herd of Thomson's gazelles, like a yo-yo at the end of its string.

Because I knew that Jesus was my Lord, Master, Savior, and God and that he would never leave me nor forsake me. He died on the cross as the final sacrifice for our sins and was resurrected on the third day so as to be the first to return alive from the sin of death started by Adam. This is why the silver cord returned me to my Boise home on Ellis Avenue. It was in order that I could pass on the good news to you.

What it means to us

God is sympathetic with people who mourn when they see people worshiping idols because in the Bible, a mark on the forehead is a symbol of a person's ownership, the Lord to whom you belong. By having their foreheads marked with the unseen sign of the cross, it shows that the person belongs to Jesus Christ, who died on the cross for us. Angels and demons see it clearly.

This is the imitation of the spiritual mark or seal that is put on a person who has accepted Jesus as their Lord, Master, Savior, and God.

Now I did not know it at the time, but in Ezekiel, it says:

> Then the LORD called to the man clothed in linen who had the writing kit at his side and said to him, "Go throughout the city of Jerusalem and put a mark on the foreheads of those who grieve and lament over all the detestable things that are done in it."
>
> As I listened, he said to the others, "Follow him through the city and kill, without showing pity or compassion. Slaughter old men, young men and maidens, women and children, but do not touch anyone who has the mark. Begin at my sanctuary."

That's when the silver cord gets busy yanking those newly dead people down to hell, the ones without the physically unseen mark, that is.

What exactly is the mark in Ezekiel 9:6?

The mark, which in Hebrew is pronounced *tāw*, is interpreted as a sign of exemption from judgment. In the Afroasiatic alphabet, it looked like an English X or the Hebrew X or *alef*, which should give Elon Musk a great deal of thought, as he uses the *X* with great zeal.

Why paganism is so bad

When I was in junior high school metal shop, I learned how to make things in the foundry by pounding sand into a metal box with a mold of the object I wanted in the middle. Once the sand was solid, I would carefully undo the mold, and the sand would have taken the form of the object I desired to make. When the mold was ready, molten aluminum was poured into the hollow mold, and when it cooled, the mold was broken open, and the object of my desire was in my hands.

With idols, there is a difference. It is formed by a craftsman, but then, the purchaser is given a list of rules of how to worship it in the hopes something magic would happen. This is clearly not possible, as it is an inanimate object with no ability to do anything.

In fact, idol worship attracts demon possession, as the place of reason within the forehead has been filled with the Pentagram of Satan instead of the Cross of Christ. So as it says, this is from the Bible and my personal experience.

My demon possession experience

While I was a member of a fellowship in Encinitas, California, they underhandedly taught me how to go OOB through NDE yoga. I learned how to do it in six weeks after fearing God and was going across the universe, or multiverse, shortly thereafter.

They taught me to focus on putting a star in the third-eye chakra (forehead, epicenter of reason). This worked for me nine-ty-nine times but ended in demon possession on the one hundredth time.

On the one hundredth time, I focused on the star in the forehead and prepared to step out, and I felt a presence that was blocking me.

When I opened my eyes, I was stunned to see a transparent alien face staring me in the eyes, and I was afraid. Then I remembered that the fellowship had told me that if I should meet a spiritual traveler, I should let it in.

I lowered the defenses that were like crossed spears, blocking it from entering. The crossed spears lowered, and then it leaped into me. Immediately, it started taking over my nervous system and took control of my body. My fists clenched so tightly, the knuckles were turning white, and I felt a superhuman strength taking over that I could not control. I felt my strength waning while it was growing stronger, so while I was still in control of my mind and voice I said, "Jesus, save me!"

A hand came out of the wall in front of me, reached into my chest and pulled out a glistening black octopus-like thing. A black hole opened up beneath the hand, the hand threw the wriggling octopus-thing into the hole, and with a wave of the hand, the hole shut and was gone. I was back in control of my own body again.

What I learned

None of this made any sense to me until after the night Christ put his hand on me and told me that I had been lied to. Then I started reading the Bible and learned about demon possession for the first time and then thought, *Oh, so that's what happened.*

The demon saw the star on the forefront of my mind and saw it as a boarding pass. It was waiting for me to step out so that it could step in. With the cross of Christ on my forehead now, they stay away because the door to my heart and mind is closed to them forever and that once it was pulled out by the hand of Jesus, it cannot bring seven worse demons along if the cross is still there. Thanks be to Jesus that I am clean.

So a question arises as to whether the silver cord is a quantum octopus of sorts that God commands to bring departed souls up or down and traveling souls back to their earthly bodies. The answer is not an easy one.

The quantum mechanics octopus, or *omnipus* rather, would have to be able to create tentacles on demand to handle all the humans exiting their bodies all around the world at any given time, rapturing some up into heaven and yanking others down to hell quickly and cleanly.

In one OOB experience, I had gone so far out into the multiverse that the silver cord was stretched to its limit to bring me back to my body on earth. This I recall quite clearly.

I have died ninety-nine times to this world under my own power through fear of God and NDE yoga but twice been OOB by God's own device called the silver cord. Once was when I asked the God of Abraham for five minutes in heaven, and the second was when I asked God for an OOB experience that I could confirm was from him.

*****

Are there levels of hell?

Could it be that hell is one level after another of flaming pits going deeper and deeper into the bowels of the earth? Is there a level of hell reserved for the worst people ever created?

My job is to show you the supernatural planes that really do exist. I have thought much about my God-given experience with the silver cord and also its functions, how it works, how it knows who to get and when, and where to put them.

So now, I will do my best to tackle the question: Does hell have levels of different punishments? Jesus talked about the rich man in hell, who said to Abraham, "I thirst." When I saw the twentieth-century rich man in hell, there was no water in his room but no fire or brimstone or darkness either. His room was clean, dry, and well-lit. All he had was his uniform and a chair to sit on. It was like a holding cell or house arrest for him alone.

There are a great deal more like him. Think of all the people who were drowned during the flood of Noah's time. Estimates run as high as six to seven billion people were on the planet at that time, and all but eight of them were pulled down to hell by the silver cord.

God did not react to my pleading for five minutes in heaven until I used the power, or *dunamus*, of Jesus's name. Indeed, God did explode with anger at me, not for asking for five minutes in heaven but for my continued rebellion against Jesus and refusal to read God's own written word, the Bible.

As it says in Matthew 12:40:

> For just as Jonah was three days and three nights
> in the belly of the whale, so for three days and

three nights the Son of Man will be in the heart
of the earth.

As Jesus is the Son of Man and the Son of God, he himself
prophesied of his own descent into Hades for three days. As it says
in 1 Peter 3 in the CJB, Paul wrote what Jesus actually did in hell:

> For the Messiah himself died for sins, once and
> for all, a righteous person on behalf of unrigh-
> teous people, so that he might bring you to God.
> He was put to death in the flesh but brought to
> life by the Spirit; and in this form he went and
> made a proclamation to the imprisoned spir-
> its, to those who were disobedient long ago, in
> the days of Noach, when God waited patiently
> during the building of the ark, in which a few
> people—to be specific, eight—were delivered by
> means of water.

He preached the good news to the rebels (or *imprisoned spirits*)
during the days of Noah that they too could see heaven if they only
repented and accepted him as their Lord, Master, Savior, and God.
Since he was down there with them in spirit, they knew he was physically dead, but at the same time, they could take hold of this one last
chance to enter heaven. And they did, all six to seven billion of them.

My visit to the rich man in the cell in hell lasted only a total
of about seven to eight minutes and was mostly a one-sided conversation. Meanwhile, my body was lying on a bed in a bedroom in
San Diego. That trip down, I do not recall the silver cord at all. But
the second time in the Ellis house, when I did actually see the silver
cord, it was pulling me backward through what felt exactly like warm
water. And at the end of 1 Peter 3, Paul said that the eight were *deliv-
ered* by means of water.

But Jesus spent three days there while his body was lying in a
tomb near Jerusalem, which is God's chosen holy city. And as it says

in the book of Revelation, the day is again coming when it will be defiled by the world's rebels.

Hell was created for Lucifer and the rebellious angels that followed him. Since Satan is still an archangel on earth in exile from heaven, he would have to be separated from those lower-ranking angels who followed him, like the way Napoleon was sent to the Isle of Elba, to stop him from recruiting another army. As history reveals, Napoleon escaped from Elba and created another army, which was finally shattered at Waterloo.

As it shows in Revelation, this is a pretty good analogy for Satan and his angels when they are released from hell after a thousand-year detention. They will meet for battle against all heaven's armies at the Valley of Megiddo—the last Waterloo?

Where did the idea of levels of hell come from?

My mom once told me about Poop Hell when I was bad: "Everyone stands in a river of sewage up to their chins. Every day at 12:00, the devil comes by on a motorboat, and everyone in the sewage screams, 'Don't make waves! Don't make waves!'" It was meant as a friendly warning for me to behave myself.

In the *Divine Comedy* by Dante Alighieri, there are levels of hell according to the sins committed. From what I have read in God's word, all sin is the breaking of God's law, but there are different punishments for each type of sin. A few examples are lust, that is, people who committed lust-driven sins like adultery and fornication; rebellion, like the souls who spoke or acted against God or the people of the one true church who comprise Jesus's body; and violence, as in those who committed violence against others and thought of committing violent acts only all the time, like in the days of Noah.

Dante's version of hell punishes the unrepentant sinner in a manner that is fitting their sins. I can't say one way or the other on that yet. Now, for those who confessed and turned away from all sins, item by item, and died with faith in Jesus as Lord, those will not be yanked down to hell by the silver cord. If you accept him as Son of Man and Son of God, first one to be resurrected from the dead, then you are raptured up to heaven by the silver cord at Jesus's command, for he has the keys to death and Hades.

Are there levels of hell?

In the New Testament, the word *gehenna* is translated as hell. There is a small valley called the Valley of Hinnom, or Gehenna, thought to be cursed because some of the kings of Judah offended God by burning their children as sacrifices to false gods in that place.

In Jeremiah 19, it says:

> Because the people have forsaken me and have profaned this place by making offerings in it to other gods whom neither they nor their fathers nor the kings of Judah have known; and because they have filled this place with the *blood of innocents*, and have built the high places of Baal to burn their sons in the fire as burnt offerings to Baal...I will make void the plans of Judah and Jerusalem

The name of this valley became a word used in the New Testament, including by the Lord Jesus, to refer to a place of torment and fire, where gehenna is translated into hell in Matthew 10:28:

> And do not fear those who kill the body but cannot kill the soul. Rather fear him who can destroy both soul and body in hell.

What does God say about hell?

Jesus spoke about why hell was created in Matthew 25:41. At the Great White Throne judgment, Jesus will say to the unfaithful, "Depart from me, you cursed, into the eternal fire prepared for the devil and his angels."

To those he sends away from his presence, Jesus says they will go to an eternal life that is really a second death in the lake of fire. He said that hell was to punish Satan *and his fallen angels*, not as a place of eternal punishment for people. So those who chose their sin over a relationship with God could not spend eternity with God, with hell becoming the only place to put them once they have experienced the first death and have only their spirit bodies left.

The rich man in hell

When I was a nineteen-year-old atheist, I did not have a father figure to speak of and so chose a historical figure who was a father type to a great multitude in twentieth-century history. After watching films in school and reading history books that included him, my heart became like his, hard as stone in pride and power.

After going to sleep one night after joining the Air Force, the next thing I knew was that I was standing in front of the gates of hell, and they opened before me. I could not cross over but was standing at attention and startled to see the very same man I had idolized, live and in person.

When he looked me in the eyes, I remembered his name. He spoke authoritatively to me, and I replied, just as Jesus had spoken about in the parable of the rich man in hell.

The book of Revelation speaks about it as the eternal destination of souls. After the millennial reign, the Lord will finally deal with Satan, putting an end to his deceit. That can be found in Revelation 20:10.

A few verses later, the apostle John wrote about the final judgment of the dead. It says, "This is the second death, the lake of fire. And if anyone's name was not found written in the book of life, he was thrown into the lake of fire."

The book of life contains all the names of the redeemed, those who put their faith in God. Other books that will be opened on that day include all the deeds a person committed. None of those deeds change the destiny of a soul that is not in the book of life, according to this passage.

Are there levels to sin?

Dante grouped people by a defining sin in his portrayal, and their punishment was appropriate to their great fault. Sin, according to him, is the by-product of giving into one's greatest weakness—their Achilles' heel.

All I have so far found is that sin is breaking of God's laws, which are guidelines for us to live successful lives. But the laws themselves cannot save, so that is why Jesus is the only way out of being snatched by the silver cord and thrown into hell.

> For as in the days before the flood, they were eating and drinking, marrying and giving in marriage, until the day that Noah entered the ark, and did not know until the flood came and took them all away. (Matthew 24:38–39)

Others believe that Earth's population was much higher. If the growth rate before the flood was like current times or 0.012, there could have been about 750 million people. But because of the long life spans and then because of the pressurized oxygen level due to the dome or *firmament* of water over the earth, the population would be much higher. Up by just 0.001 would put the population to less than five billion.

The judgment of the flood caught people unaware, just as the coming judgment (2 Peter 3) will fall on a world that does not expect it. Earth currently has about seven billion inhabitants. How many of them will be judged with eternal condemnation if the Lord were to return like tomorrow?

We must share the gospel of Jesus Christ while we still have the opportunity, and AiG's Evangelistic Ark, opening July 7 in Northern Kentucky, will reach millions of souls with the gospel.

So yes, God has created OOB purposes for a very definite reason, to know that we are not walking, talking creatures descended from apes that have no existence after death. I hope I have proved this ad infinitum. It is also to create a quasi-memorable barrier between this temporary physical realm and the permanent world to come.

So our travels through existence start from a soul being called from the spirit realm and into a child in the womb. Then the person is born and lives a life in the world, and then comes death and the destination of heaven or hell by the silver cord, strictly according to what the person put their faith into at time of death.

With psychology 101 came the theory that the brain is just a machine running on low electrical energy to keep you aware and functioning in the world around you until you die. But this is a half-truth.

OOB experiences are to be treasured by us as reminders that we are eternal beings with citizenship in heaven who have a short life in this world. Our lives are to be used to glorify Jesus first and then live our lives second—God, country, and family, as was the tradition of our greatest generation.

When Jesus said for us to be *fishers of men*, he was referring to the fact that when you die, the silver cord is what will be used to reel you up into heaven as if on a cross. For I recalled that the same speed in which I was pulled up in heaven is the same speed at which the silver cord pulled me down through the earth to hover above the plains of the Serengeti.

This thought connection, laden with portent, had been given to me while I wrote this part of the book, as God *through the Holy Spirit* keeps these key points hidden, until you start really doing what He wants you to do. That is, to glorify him, magnify him, and show the world his perfection and greatness.

To keep and preserve this cord, that is, to keep yourself alive in Christ, you must walk in God's desire of what you are thinking and doing. God works the unseen potter's wheel, which you are standing on, the potter's wheel on which I was standing on in heaven, which God rotated left and right so I could see the New Jerusalem once and the tree of life three times and glorify Adonai, Yeshua, and the Ruach HaKodesh in front of his throne twice from a distance of about fifteen feet.

As it says in Isaiah 64:8:

> And yet, O Lord, you are our Father. We are the
> clay and you are the potter. We are all formed by
> your hand.

When I was in the second year of middle school, I met a new friend in art class. He and I were goofing off by making toys out of the wet clay the instructor had given us. We were supposed to make clay bowls, but instead, we turned the clay into laser pistols and pretended to shoot each other with them. "Pew, pew, pew!"

"Stop that at once!" the teacher yelled. "You are making me so very angry!" His face was turning red. My art class friend later became a famous actor in the *Star Wars* saga. I had no idea at the time who he would become, but I can tell you that we both got a *C* in that art class.

*****

As Paul the apostle wrote, "Focus on that which is good, clean, pure, wholesome, and of a good report." That is what you must focus on and do. Select each word Paul said therein, and find a frame of mind that will stay with you to be good. Good is not subjective, but what the Bible says.

So find what things are good in the Bible, and think about those things and then what things are clean, then what things are pure, then what things are wholesome, and what biblical things that are of a good report. Fearing God, for example, is where I started with what is biblically *good*. That is the same moment as when Adonai shouted, "Yes, I AM!", through the black hole and right to my face. That was my first step in the right direction.

Another good first-step example would be what to do about cursing. Is it really that bad, and what harm does it do?

When I was in grade school, I heard a George Carlin skit entitled *Shoot*. It was all about the *S* word, and it made me laugh pretty hard. After using that word whenever the right situation arose, I found that it did relieve some tension but also made me angry and made me feel more powerful.

Then I used the *F* word for the first time, and I noticed that it degraded me on the inside. When I was biking through a group of kids waiting for the bus, one of them grabbed the handle on the back seat of my bike. "F——R!" I shouted. Then I sped off. Once again, the word degraded me, and I stopped using it altogether.

On this, Paul the apostle said in Colossians 3:

> Away then with sinful, earthly things; deaden the evil desires lurking within you; have nothing to do with sexual sin, impurity, lust, and shameful desires; don't worship the good things of life, for that is idolatry. God's terrible anger is upon those who do such things. You used to do them when your life was still part of this world; but now is the time to cast off and throw away all these rotten garments of anger, hatred, cursing, and dirty language.

So how did that apply to me as an atheist? I rejected pornography as I saw that it was not good for me; in fact, I realized it was a lie. Looking at a picture with a magnifying glass, you will see the image is actually a collection of colored dots called *pixels*. Photos can be altered, further distorting the lie.

I rejected drugs, though I grew up in San Diego, and I did notice that many people around me were into one form of drug or another. Once again, I recognized that it was pure folly.

*****

There was a wealthy engineer who had just retired and had a large house. His son came back from college and told his father about a drug, and so the whole family started smoking it. Then they all had a drug-induced brainstorm that they would sell everything they had and buy an RV and drive down to the jungles of Brazil to shell coconuts for a living. As they drove through the dirt roads in the jungles of Brazil, the RV was so long, large, and heavy that it was damaged many times on sharp rocks and got stuck in mud pits. When they reached the coconut plantation, they found out that they would only make a few pennies for many pounds of shelled coconuts. So they returned to the USA with nothing. Moral of the story: drugs make you stupid and ruin your life, while the drug dealers collect all the money.

When I was nine, a relative had offered me a cigarette. I took one puff and started coughing badly. "Smoking cigarettes is stupid," I said, flicking the damn thing away. I never smoked anything again.

There is one time when I had an altered view of what was really going on because the doctor gave me a sedative. While I was stationed at Minot AFB, I had to have my wisdom teeth pulled out, so the Air Force dentist gave me a codeine IV while I was lying on the chair.

After a few minutes, I was feeling kind of spacey, and then he produced a pair of pliers. "Let's have a look at that tooth," he said, putting the pliers in my mouth. I felt a pinprick in my jaw, and he produced a bloody molar with his pliers.

"Well, lookee there," he said. "Now, let's try the other one." Another pinprick on the other side of my jaw produced another bloody molar. "You'll have to stay here till it wears off. The nurse will show you to your room," he said, smiling.

As I lay in the hospital bed, I watched a very long and boring cartoon on the TV. When the codeine wore off, I suddenly realized I was not watching a cartoon but the summer Olympics.

CHAPTER 6

Your Perfect Body

While I spent my five minutes in heaven, the first part of it was spent rocketing upward that felt faster than the speed of sound. The perfect joy had already entered me right after I had been sucked into the mouth of the whirlwind. I still recall how I was wearing a very thin and light robe. The robe barely touched my skin, and the sleeves ended at the wrists, but did not touch the skin. It was always just above the skin throughout my entire visit to heaven. After I had gone through to the cloud level of the third heaven, I hovered there for a moment being held aloft by an unseen force (the silver cord). My arms were out to the left and right and my legs straight down as if on an invisible cross. All I could think was, "Whatever God has in me for me." Then my body was moved forward by that unseen force, and my toes were pointing down to just a few inches above the cirrus cloud layer. The superfast rapture journey upward felt the same as when the silver cord pulled me downward in my years-later OOB travel to the Serengeti.

How did I feel when I got to the third heaven? Full of joy and an anticipation of trust that God would provide for me a full visit to heaven. When I saw the brown jasper wall of heaven appear on the horizon with three giant pearls stuck in it, my joy and anticipation were unchanged. I had only one thought, "Whatever God has in mind for me."

Drifting through the giant *Pearl Gate* as mentioned in Revelation 22 did not feel any different than going through a mist, even though the giant pearl *appeared* solid. The moment I went through to the other side of the gate, my feet touched ground abruptly, but not

"

harshly. I was immediately aware of my feet, ankles, and legs again. My arms went down to my sides, as gravity took over again.

I could see all the people who were in white robes and walking to the left and right. They all had different types of hair as common to human nature, as they looked up at the blue sky with their arms crossed across their chests. And they raised their hands in the air to praise God because, as it says in 1 Timothy 2:8:

> When we lift our hands to Heaven, we therefore present everything we are, everything we have done, and everything we have to God.

The people in the white robes also had different skin and hair types. Then I saw the outline of the New Jerusalem, which was gold, and the houses appeared to be twenty feet tall on average and higher. I did see a golden temple with a rounded dome there too, but just the outline.

That is when I was turned to the right to look at the Tree of Life. In a lush-green valley about a mile and a half away, there was a huge tree with a white trunk in the middle of a river. When I looked up that tree to try to see the top of it, that is when I felt a little tug at the back of my robe and at the small of my back, the same place where the silver cord would wrap around the base of my spine ten years later.

Does it hold up to Revelation?

I did see angelic persons with large brownish wings in light-blue robes flying up to the Tree of Life and then bringing down armloads of fruit and giving them to the people below. As it says in Revelation 22, "And on each side of the river, there was the Tree of Life, which bore twelve crops of fruit, a different kind every month." What I recall was seeing the Tree of Life in the middle of a river in a green valley.

Now Revelation 22 says:

> Next the angel showed me the river of the water of
> life, sparkling like crystal, flowing from the throne
> of God and of the Lamb. Between the main street
> and the river was the Tree of Life producing twelve
> kinds of fruit, a different kind every month; and
> the leaves of the tree were for healing the nations—
> no longer will there be any curses. The throne of
> God and of the Lamb will be in the city, and his
> servants will worship him; they will see his face,
> and his name will be on their foreheads.

To the right of Christ's throne, I did catch a glimpse of a huge throne with water flowing from the seat of it but did not see how it flowed to the valley. I was not able to look down or move about, and all my motion was controlled by an unseen force (God's hands) that turned the potter's wheel I was standing on left or right.

I could look ahead and up and lift my hands to praise God while I stood to the left side of his throne. This means that I was standing on the side of his right hand as he was facing me, though I could not see him because of the brightness of his shekinah glory. I had to be standing at his right hand as he faced me because the second time I glorified him, I saw the back left foot of his beryl throne and the right armrest. This means he was sitting on the throne to let me glorify him the first time and was standing to receive me the second time.

The bright white light I looked into was God's shekinah glory, which was also manifested during the transfiguration in Matthew 17: "As they watched, He began to change form—His face shone like the sun, and His clothing became as white as light." This means that Jesus was radiating the perfect light from the whole of himself, and that light was brighter than the sun.

For Revelations 22 says:

> There will be no more night, they will not need
> the light of a lamp or the light of the sun for the

Lord God is the light. And they will reign for ever
and ever.

On reflecting the yellow light that comes out hot from a summer sun versus seeing the bluish-white shekinah light that radiates
throughout heaven, I have to say that the bluish-white light of Christ
is clean and does not radiate heat. It provides a cleanliness of sight
and a sense of joy from knowing there is no darkness.

Going back to the silver cord, God had Moses and Elijah lowered from heaven (a.k.a. Abraham's bosom in Christ's time and
before), using the unseen silver cord for the Transfiguration.

As it shows again in Acts 1:10–11:

> They were looking intently up into the sky as he
> was going, when suddenly two men dressed in
> white stood beside them. "Men of Galilee," they
> said, "why do you stand here looking into the
> sky? This same Jesus, who has been taken from
> you into heaven, will come back in the same way
> you have seen him go into heaven."

The purpose of the Transfiguration was for several reasons, to
reveal Jesus to us in his full glory, so that we are changed to glorify
him on this earth. The significance of Moses and Elijah appearing
before Jesus at his Transfiguration is because they are the epiphany of
death, judgment, and the final destiny of our souls. And it draws par-
allels between Jesus and two of the greatest prophets in God's Word
and also for you to recognize God's voice from heaven, "This is my
beloved Son: hear him" (Mark 9:7).

The white robe peeps

Why were the people in the white robes walking around the city
with their arms crossed over their chests?

It is a comforting, self-soothing pose that helps you concentrate
and stay focused on the breathless, delightful joy you experience.

And as for stopping and praising God, Jesus, and the Holy Spirit three times at seemingly random intervals, I can only say that they do it out of pure loving enchanted spontaneity.

The white robes people in heaven were the ones on the south side of the city, and there were three rows. The row in the foreground was going west, the second row was going east, and the line in the background was going west. It makes me think of the battle of Jericho, as the Jews were marching around the city of Jericho with the ark of the covenant led by seven priests with shofars.

So which direction is heaven?

When I was raptured up to heaven, I was facing north, when I was just above the striated cirrus cloud layer. I was carried along by the silver cord to the southern center pearl gate, as it says in Job 26:7:

> He stretches out the north over empty space
> And hangs the earth on nothing.

There is a *void* in the north of our universe. This empty spot has been found by observatories across the globe, starting with the one on Mount Palomar near Escondido, California. I have climbed that mountain several times to see the observatory myself.

In Job 37:22, it says:

> Out of the north comes golden splendor;
> Around God is awesome majesty.

But the people walking around the golden city (see map) were in white robes on their own with no weapons or shofars and no ark or Levitical priests. I believe the original ark is in the temple in the city center, which appeared to be on a low hill.

As Jesus said:

> You are the light of the world. A city on a hill
> cannot be hidden. Neither do people light a lamp
> and put it under a bowl.

What about the Tree of Life?

Revelation 22 says, "And the leaves of the tree were for the healing of the nations. No longer will there be any curse."

The leaves I saw on the Tree of Life were round and about one foot across. They were green on one side and gold on the other. In the Bible, God uses gold as the protector of wealth, a sacred store of value that transcends time and is everlasting.

Our current use of man-made paper money and digital currency represents instability, a lack of virtue, and encourages living wastefully in excess. The use of gold by individuals as well as nations will lead us on a path where we can arrive at a wealth approved by God. A wealth of nations and of brotherhood born out of the crucible of discipline, restraint, and integrity. The heat of the fires of testing in the crucible's furnace will bring the dross of our hearts to the surface for God to scrape off to make us his lambs of purest gold and of the finest quality. To make it through this furnace of testing, it is best to pray for God to keep a hedge of protection around you every day (Job 1). And then, put on the full armor of God as prescribed by Paul.

As for the green side of the leaves of the Tree of Life, we go to Jeremiah 17:

> Blessed in the man who trusts in Adonai, he will
> be like a tree planted by the waters: His leaf shall
> be green; and he shall not be anxious in the year of
> drought, neither shall he cease from yielding fruit.

So we can gather from this that the green leaf denotes the truth of faith, the faith which is from the charity of the Tree of Life. The green of the leaves also gives fertility, abundance, growth, peace, victory, and rebirth. These are the things we can hope for through faith in God that he will heal our nations. In prayer, you can ask God for him to send a leaf from the Tree of Life to heal and restore our nation.

And we must remember that Jesus was killed on a tree stripped of its roots and branches. It consisted of two wooden sections, one vertical and one horizontal. He had to die on the cross for the forgiveness of our breaking of God's laws, which were put into writing on the tablets God gave to Moses, not to mention the covenants that preceded the tablets, starting with Adam and Eve. That is what I had been in ignorance of for so many years, and so though we may be in want of many things, beware of ignorance, which can destroy your immortality in heaven. You do not want your name erased from the Lamb's Book of Life.

Trees are mentioned in the Bible more than any living thing other than God and human beings. We need to be like trees planted by streams of water that yield their fruit in season. This is because the roots of a tree go all the way down to life-giving water while anchoring itself into the earth, giving it growth and stability. Jesus said he is the true vine and that his Father is the dresser of the garden. And the Bible refers to itself as a Tree of Life in Proverbs 3, "She (wisdom from God) is a tree of life to them that lay hold upon her: and happy is everyone that retains her (Memorizes God's Word)."

God is always trying to teach us to think long term. Moreover, every major prophet in the Bible appears in conjunction with a tree. Noah received the olive branch from a dove, Abraham sat under the oaks of Mamre, and Joseph is no exception, as the Bible tells us that Joseph *is* a tree, meaning that from Joseph (who was a preincarnate Christ) was the tree from which Israel grew into a mighty nation (from the spreading of fruit).

The same pattern holds true in the New Testament, as a vertically challenged taxman named Zacchaeus climbed a sycamore tree so that he could see over the crowds and view Jesus coming. When you have a strong heart for seeing the works of God in action, God will provide opportunities for you to join the bandwagon.

The apostle Paul asserted that if we have gone for a walk in the woods, we are without excuse for knowing God. Like me on my long drive from Mississippi to California, I came to understand that there was no way the natural order of the world could have been from an accident. It had to be a pre-established design that was completely thought out from beginning to end. So nature is a form of general revelation that God created all things. That is how those who refuse to read the Bible or accept Christ as their Lord, Master, Savior, and God will be judged.

Paul also wrote that the faithful are like branches grafted into Israel's tree trunk, replacing those who have separated themselves from Christ. The Tree of Life is a cultivated tree with branches of different fruit trees grafted in so that it can bear many kinds of fruit, which is along the lines of why I could not approach the Tree of Life in heaven. I had not yet been grafted in or had the roots that help us stand fast against the storms of worldly adversaries.

In the apocryphal book *Apocalypse of Moses*, it says that Seth and his mother, Eve, went back to the Gates of Paradise to retrieve a vial of the *Oil of Mercy* from the Tree of Life. This was because Adam, who was dying at the ripe old age of 946, was sick and dying. But the Archangel Michael said, "Seth, man of God, weary not thyself of prayers and entreaties concerning the tree that flows with oil to anoint thy father Adam. For it shall not be yours now, but in the end times."

So the three main things that were crucial for me to be considered by God to visit heaven were threefold:

1. Have faith in Jesus's name at least the size of a grain of mustard seed.
2. Destroy your faith in all your good works before God.
3. Beg for it if you have to, for God dismisses the words of the proud, but the humble he will hear.

And so it is with us who believe and know.

CHAPTER 7
Planting a Church

Why am I including this subject in a book on what God has done for me? Because I have spent most of my life like *Ebeneezer Scrooge*, who was a fictional character of Charles Dickens that I chose as a thirteen-year-old atheist to emulate. Scrooge's miserly life was taken from a real-life person named James Wood, who was one of the richest men in London in the 1830s. James was so stingy that he wore the same clothes every day and would not give so much as a penny to a starving mother and her baby. He never broke the law, but he did violate every financially moral rule of thumb so as to make enemies of everyone in Victorian London.

On the night before Christmas, he died, and the whole of London turned up to jeer, taunt, and curse the horse-drawn funeral wagon that paraded his body through the cobblestone streets. Some even got onto the wagon to jump upon and kick his coffin, as in the musical version of *Scrooge* with Albert Finney.

But why did Scrooge withhold money from the poor and lord it over his debtors? Control and separation from hope. Just as I have been mostly silent of God's special intercessions and corrections in my life, Scrooge withheld money from those who needed it most. Even so, God disciplines those whom he loves, and so I have finally reached the point of actually teaching God's Word right down to where the rubber meets the road.

So after inquiring with my pastor who is a church planter, starting a church and then keeping it going is a calling from God. Like Paul the apostle being told by the Holy Spirit where to go and what to do, we are to follow his lead and fulfill his desire for the church body.

After Christ put his hand on my right shoulder and I knew I had to put my faith into God's written word, I then started applying the Bible to my life. Going to different churches starting with Assembly of God and then getting baptized and tithing and giving to the poor were the beginnings of growth in my new life.

If C. S. Lewis had started a church, what would it be called? Why he did not do any church planting is a puzzle to me, as he and I had similar atheism-to-faith beginnings. Clive Lewis had rejected Christianity in his early teens and lived as an atheist through his twenties. While fighting in the trenches of World War I, he swore he would never bend the knee to pray, me too, but it was many decades later and in the Air Force.

He preached several times at the University Church of St. Mary's. On Sundays, he worshiped at his parish church, called the Holy Trinity. He came to faith in God in 1931 through logic, with the help of his close friend and devout Roman Catholic, J. R. R. Tolkien, the creator of *The Lord of the Rings*. But for some unknown reason, he did not do any church planting.

To go back to my experience with the silver cord and Billy Graham, among other evangelicals, is my cross to bear. As Jesus said, in Matthew 10:38, "Those who do not take up their cross and follow in my steps are not fit to be my disciples."

Back to the light

And the lamp I was circling around in my Ellis house was not a physical object but a spiritual one. The lamp cannot be seen by the naked eye. As it says in Revelation 1:20:

> As for the mystery of the seven stars which you saw in My right hand, and the seven golden lampstands: the seven stars are the angels of the seven churches, and the seven lampstands are the seven churches.

Now we know that the seven lampstands are symbolic of seven first churches. The seven stars have been translated as to be the pastors of the seven churches. But the meaning of the two lampstands changes in Revelation 11:

> And I will grant authority to my two witnesses, and they will prophesy for twelve hundred and sixty days, clothed in sackcloth. These are the two olive trees and the two lampstands that stand before the Lord of the earth.

So we must read the context in order to understand what is occurring. In Revelation 11, the two lampstands refer to the two witnesses that God will send during the last half of the tribulation period. That is the seven-year event we want to miss altogether through the rapture.

When I graduated high school, I was given a marble and told to give it to the principal when I shook his hand. This was a secret game between the graduation class and the principal, to see how much of a bulge of marbles his trouser pocket would have at the end of the ceremony. But I kept the marble, and he looked at me funny.

Upon entering heaven

After going through the assigned pearl gate, Jesus will give us a white stone with a new name as he said to John in the Isle of Patmos in Revelation 2:17.

What Christ may say to each person entering and approaching his greenish-white beryl throne of the bema judgment is, "Well done, good and faithful servant." Then he gives you a white stone with a new name that only you know.

In ancient Greece, jury members gave a white stone to show acquittal. Also, principal buildings were made of white marble, like the temple of Asclepius in Pergamum. Its white marble pillars were engraved with the names of people that had been healed by God, like the miracle healing I received while running to meet the Idaho Air Guard 1.5-mile time requirements.

So the white stone with the believer's name written on it shows our standing in God's presence. But white stone may be a translucent precious stone like a diamond. The word *white* in the Greek Septuagint is *leukos* and can also mean *sparkling* and *bright*. In ancient Jerusalem, the high priest or *Cohen Gadol* wore an ephod breastplate with twelve different stones mounted in gold filigree. Each different stone represents a tribe of Israel. The sixth one was a rock crystal or *diamond* for the tribe of Naphtali.

So we must remember what Jesus Christ said about this in John 10, "I am the gate; whoever enters through me will be saved." So through faith in him alone, not works, we can then enter the realm of God.

More on running

There is also a Roman custom of awarding white stones to the victors of athletic games. The winner was awarded a white stone with his name inscribed on it. This served as his ticket to a banquet.

As Paul said about running a victory race in 2 Timothy 4:7, "I have fought the good fight, I have finished the race, I have kept the faith."

Jesus gives the overcomers entrance to the eternal victory celebration in heaven and the marriage supper of the lamb.

The meaning of the spiritual hanging lamp

The lampstands were symbolic of Christ's light shining and piercing a spiritually dark world. Churches and pastors are to be examples of supreme holiness in a world where Satan spreads the darkness of lies and murder even though he is an angel of light. This I have seen for myself. When Satan entered into my darkened prayer room to accuse me before God with a scepter in his right hand, he glowed with the same luminescence as starlight, for his name is

Lucifer, the son of the morning star, the morning star being Venus. He has the same glow as starlight, like the light of a full moon.

His original title was the praise and worship leader of God and was archangel Lucifer, until his great wisdom begot pride and pride begot rebellion. His rebellion was probably in response to God one day allowing us to judge the angels.

Paul said it in 1 Corinthians 6:3:

> Don't you know that we will judge angels, not to
> mention affairs of everyday life?

Jesus is the bright and morning star, which would be like sunlight that outshines all other created light. That would be the shekinah glory that radiates from God and Christ in perfect purity. The same light I saw radiating from the Beryl Throne in heaven.

All material things in this world are made of energy, as Einstein stated in $E=MC^2$. Energy equals matter times the speed of light (3.00×10^8 Meters Per Second) to the second power. So to have some fun with it, imagine that your superpower was that you could throw a baseball faster than the speed of light. On a clear night sky, you aim for the horsehead nebula, wind up for the pitch, and let it soar. As the ball goes faster and faster to the speed of light, it stretches and becomes the full light spectrum of red, yellow, green, and blue. The tail end of the spectrum is red because red is the slowest. The front of the spectrum is blue because blue is the fastest. Then, the baseball loses all its form and returns to the natural state of protons, neutrons, and electrons.

The angel of Austin

How can angels go through walls? Why does God send angels to visit us? Questions like those did not even occur to me until after I saw a real angel when I woke up in my hotel room—while I was a field service engineer in Austin, Texas. And this is how it came about.

While working one day in Austin Texas, installing a multimillion dollar robotic workstation for my company, I went to the hotel on a hill after the twelve-hour shift. While lying down on my bed and watching the news, a woman reporter stated that two cars were racing down south Lamar street when one car jumped the curb and crushed a woman waiting at a bus stop. Then, I heard the reporter say, "When people gathered around her, someone stole the dead woman's purse." I became frightened for my own life, though I was on the top level of a four-story hotel.

So I ran to the door and bolted it, closed the curtains, and shut off all the lights. Lying there in my bed, I tossed and turned until I got out of bed and knelt down. I begged God fervently to watch over me closely that night. All I wanted to do was wake up alive in the morning. I tossed and turned in the cold darkness until I somehow fell asleep.

When I awoke, I noticed a funny light blue on the ceiling. When I looked to the foot of my bed, I saw a translucent woman standing there in a light-blue robe with a bright light radiating from her face. The light from her face was so bright that I could not see her face but saw her beautiful electric-blue eyes.

She looked up at my legs, and our eyes met. Then she knew I was awake and walked to the left side of my bed. She looked down at me as if to say, "Do you remember me?"

I looked up to her as if to say, "Oh yes, I remember you." Then she turned around to show me her light-brown feathery wings that were like a sparrow's. They arched up from her shoulders to her head and were so long, the wing tips almost touched the ground. Then she walked away from me and went straight through the wall, between the lamp on the left and the TV on the right.

It is my sneaking suspicion the silver cord sneaks up on you if you're going to hell, as I had no idea of the silver cord when I was an atheist. I was pulled down to the gates of hell unconsciously, as I don't recall that pull down at all, just the arrival at the black gates of hell.

The multicolored hanging Tiffany-style stained glass lamp that I was hovering around was on the northeastern edge of the ceiling between the archway, the living room, and dining room of my house on Ellis in Boise, Idaho. It looked just like a Meyda Tiffany

Hanginghead Dragonfly Shade, but without the dragonflies. The bits of glass were different shapes and sizes of green, blue, yellow, and red. I hovered around it in a counterclockwise direction, praising God and glorifying him to the lamp to give encouragement to the churches. Just as there are many styles of teaching the Bible to different peoples and cultures, there were differing shapes and colors of glass in the Tiffany-style shade.

After much prayer and biblical insight, the meaning has become clear. Like Billy Graham whose cross it was to bear by bringing the hope of Christ circling around the darkening churches of the world, so must I. So must we all, whether through the Internet or live in church evangelism or church planting after much prayer and group prayer, and then you may find your *calling*.

The lamp represents the churches of today that are dim to God's Word right now, as the wattage rating in the lamp was too weak to show through the vast array of beautiful colors it was supposed to give off. Much of this is teaching only bits and pieces of the Bible out of context to please the itching ears of the congregants. Everyone needs to read the Bible in its entirety, as I have done so myself many times over.

I cannot recommend going to the cemetery (I mean seminary college), as they are teaching dead religion. God does not listen to repetitious prayers with no real passion in them. No theatrical prayers for me, just a *soul call* encased in love that is sent to God with a patient fortitude to await his response. That is what I do, as I cannot do it any other way. I have to be real with God, and this could be your catchphrase also.

A soul call is similar to what Jesus called a *b'rakhah*, a calling out to God with thanksgiving. The biblical version of a soul call comes from Samuel:

> Eli said to her, "How long are you going to stay
> drunk? Stop drinking your wine!" But Hannah
> answered, "No, my lord, I am a very unhappy
> woman. I have not drunk either wine or other

strong liquor; rather, I've been *pouring out my soul* before ADONAI."

And did God hear her soul call? Yes, he gave her fertility, and she bore a son, whom she dedicated to serve God at the temple. His name was Samuel, and he became a mighty man of God. Then she had other children afterward to raise as her own.

I asked God which version of the Bible he wanted me to read, and while I was walking around Barnes and Nobles, I stopped at the Bible section and was moved by the Holy Spirit to take out and look at a Complete Jewish Bible. After reading some of the scriptures while sipping coffee, I found it to be like driving a Rolls-Royce *Silver Shadow* on a road paved with gold and lined with beautiful trees, with mountains in the distance.

When I looked at the price, I was taken aback as I was on a tight budget. Then I said to God that if he really wanted me to get that Bible, he should let me find one at a lower price. Lo and behold, when I was walking around a secondhand store, there on the book-shelf was a brand-new CJB for five dollars. I bought it and started reading it the moment I got home.

This was because the CJB read true to God's original intent by the unedited hand of the pens of the prophets. It goes to the original interpretations of the rabbis and bypasses the archaic King James language altogether. It uses modern English and also teaches critical Hebrew words here and there, with a glossary in the back.

The apostle Paul was taught by the Holy Spirit, so it is with me. With the guidance of the Holy Spirit, I read through the KJV twice, one PEV until it fell apart, the Catholic Bible with the Apocrypha, and the CJB over five times. Now, I am reading my grandmother's KJV and gaining insight to the footnotes she wrote here and there next to passages in her Bible. My sister had it for twenty-five years and never read it and then just gave it to me. She has no faith in God that I know of, and I have found it impossible to talk to her on that subject.

Reading the KJV for the first time was like driving an old car with a bad suspension on fifty miles of bad road. The road was filled with potholes, speedbumps, and confusing road signs.

But I was determined to get through it and understood that every word was true. The Holy Spirit was watching and making sure of that. No one interfered with my daily reading, and I had a great many questions that needed answers. So I did go to churches and gained more insight into scripture.

So we are the lamps of God to shine brightly as pastors, priests, prophets, and God's men and women. This is my cross to bear, as I swore as an atheist that I would never have anything to do with Christ or the Bible. But as Jesus said in Matthew 21:28:

> "What do you think? A man had two sons. He went to the first and said, 'Son, go and work in the vineyard today.' The boy answered, 'I will not.' But later he had a change of heart and went. The father went to the other son and said the same thing. This boy answered, 'I will, sir,' but did not go. Which of the two did his father's will?"
>
> They said, "The first."
>
> Jesus said to them, "I tell you the truth, tax collectors and prostitutes will go ahead of you into the kingdom of God! For John came to you in the way of righteousness, and you did not believe him. But the tax collectors and prostitutes believed him. Although you saw this, you did not later change your minds and believe him."

As it was with me, after years of running away from my assigned task, I finally turned around and said, "Okay, Lord, here I am to do your will."

Type of church to start

I have been to a lot of different churches here in Idaho and found strengths and weaknesses in almost all of them. The usual weakness is not teaching the Bible in context, giving only occasional parts of the Bible, trying to say there is no rapture, which requires removing or misquoting parts of the Bible or twisting scripture in strange ways. That is how people esigete the Bible, that is, to interpret it in such a way as to suit their own purposes. This can be prevented by going down to the original meaning of the writer of the passage or *context*.

How to select a Bible that suits you

The first Bible I read was a KJV because it was given to me by a person I respected. I kept it high on a shelf, but did not read it until the day after Christ put his hand on my left shoulder and said, "You have been lied to." In other words, the world's religious system had deceived me.

So after reading the KJV twice, it was very hard for me to get a complete picture of the entirety of its contents. So I asked God what version of the Bible he wanted me to use, as I trust God completely and in all subjects.

At one church that I attended twice, they were passing around the offering basket while singing half-heartedly. I was taken aback by their weak performance, looked up, and said, "Lord, Lord, what is going on with this church?"

He replied, "They are neither hot nor cold."

While I was in Biloxi, Mississippi, I did go to a Baptist church for the first time. The fire and brimstone teaching of the preacher there was inspiring, but it did not last. The seed fell on a hard path, as the teachings of the world had trodden on my heart, making it callous to God's Word.

The Assembly of God church I went to in Meridian was very good. In that church one Sunday in 2004, I went to the front and prayed with a woman and then saw the Holy Spirit for the first time.

I went to the front of the congregation for an altar call, where there were three well-dressed man and wife couples receiving people and one woman in a T-shirt and jeans standing all alone. I prayed with her about my book publication, and while we prayed, I was compelled to look over my left shoulder. I saw the Holy Spirit drifting down from the upper-left corner of the church's ceiling. It looked like a transparent silken parachute with a cowl on top, but no face, and it drifted down slowly until it landed on us, as gently as a dove.

One question kept running in the back of my mind from time to time: *Why did the Holy Spirit land on both of us?* The answer did not come to me until three years later. She was a single woman, and I was supposed to get married to her.

At that church, they did allow one woman to speak in tongues and then interpret. When the whole congregation was silent in prayer, she wailed, and in tears, she spoke. I could tell it was real inspiration from the Holy Spirit. The last time she did so, she said in anger, "And this church had better start getting it right!"

My only experience in speaking in tongues happened exactly as it happened on the day of Pentecost. While I was working in a temporary position to make ends meet, I had to take small boxes of select bars from a large cardboard box so that the smaller boxes could be taken apart and the bars put into even smaller boxes. A Muslim coworker from Bosnia was sitting in front of me, and as I continued emptying the bigger boxes, I started delighting myself in the Lord. I became so enamored with the Lord that I forgot what I was doing.

I had a stack of flattened boxes resting on my forearms, and I said to him, "What do I do with these boxes?"

He was shocked and said, "I didn't know that you knew how to speak Bosnian!"

"I don't know how to speak Bosnian," I replied.

"You're speaking Bosnian right now!" he said.

*****

On the day of Pentecost, the church members were overwhelmed by the Holy Spirit and talked in the dialects of the outsiders, causing them great consternation.

Below is the prayer of Hannah in 1 Samuel:

> ADONAI kills and makes alive; he brings down to the grave, and he brings up. ADONAI makes poor, and he makes rich; he humbles, and he exalts. He raises the poor from the dust, lifts up the needy from the trash pile; he gives them a place with leaders and assigns them seats of honor. For the earth's pillars belong to ADONAI; on them he has placed the world.

So this will be my cross to bear, to mainly evangelize as I had seen Billy Graham do while I was an atheist and to help plant churches in these last days of the Age of the Gentiles.

The foundation is truth

When Pontious Pilate asked Jesus what is truth, he was not asking what it was. He was saying that truth was subjective and twistable to whatever your needs were for the moment. This is not so, as Paul the apostle said, "A half-truth is a whole lie."

That which is not based on facts is deception. As Paul the apostle said in 1 Corinthians 9–14:

> For we are God's servants, working together; you are God's field, God's building. According to the grace of God given to me, like a skilled master builder I laid a foundation, and someone else is building on it. Each builder must choose with care how to build on it. For no one can lay any foundation other than the one that has been laid; that foundation is Jesus Christ. Now if anyone builds on the foundation with gold, silver,

> precious stones, wood, hay, straw—the work of each builder will become visible, for the Day will disclose it, because it will be revealed with fire, and the fire will test what sort of work each has done. If what has been built on the foundation survives, the builder will receive a reward.

From this passage, we learn that I had been building a fortress of darkness that was tested by Christ putting his hand on me and gently telling me the truth—thus putting my building to the test. The fire of "the Day" tested my skyscraper of worldly wisdom and blew it up. It collapsed, failing the test of fire completely, as will all skyscrapers of worldly wisdom and false religion, which are built of wood, hay, and stubble that burns up and then falls to ashes. And the foundation of folly—be it Big Bang theory, evolution, or whatever upon which they are built—will be shattered.

Now, the grace of God has used Paul to build a new foundation in me. He is a skilled master builder who laid the new foundation, which is God's Word, with Christ being the perfect cornerstone.

Truth is based upon facts, which are set fast in the stone foundation of objective reality. From middle school on into the Air Force, I was repetitiously taught the truth tables required by logic circuits. "If, then" and other simple logic statements are easily employed by biblical standards as they require logical input and irrefutable facts.

Bill Gates once said, "Garbage in, garbage out." This means that if you enter lies and other trash into the system, you will have to toss the answer onto the rubbish heap, like when I heard the first Bible teaching from a fellowship I joined in Leucadia, near Carlsbad, California. A preacher in an orange robe stood behind a podium and said, "You know that Jesus preached reincarnation because he said, 'In my father's house, there are many mansions.'"

The moment I heard him say it, I knew he was wrong and had twisted it. But everyone else in the little ivy-covered cottage of a church was nodding their heads in acceptance. Even though I was refusing the Bible at the time, I believe that the Holy Spirit was guiding me in truth and logic to see through the fallacy of his teaching.

On the following Sunday, the preacher said, "You can do any-thing you want, and God will never be angry with you."

I knew that was also a lie because when I asked God to give me five minutes in heaven in Jesus's name, he said to me, "Be you still! And be prepared to receive a gift from heaven your body *cannot* contain!"

His voice was angry, and he was *shouting*. The loud bang was from God clapping his hands one time to appease his anger against me instead of destroying me. I attribute God's mercy on me because I had used Jesus's name, though my faith was the size of a grain of mustard seed. In Matthew 17:20, Jesus said:

> Because you have such little trust! Yes! I tell you
> that if you have trust as tiny as a mustard seed,
> you will be able to say to this mountain, "Move
> from here to there!" and it will move; indeed,
> nothing will be impossible for you!

So a church requires irrefutable facts based on inexhaustible research of God's Word. This means getting to the original writings of the authors who wrote the sixty-six books of the Bible when nec-essary. In today's world, this is relatively easy, as there are many Bible websites that can be found with just a few words in the search bar.

How to be an ambassador for God

As Paul the apostle said, "Dear friends, I urge you as aliens and temporary residents not to give in to the desires of your old nature, which keep warring against you." Second Corinthians 5:17 of the CJB says:

> Therefore, if anyone is united with the Messiah,
> he is a new creation - the old has passed; look,
> what has come is fresh and new!

So what are the responsibilities of an ambassador? Ambassadors are top-notch diplomats representing their home country while maintaining good relationships with other countries. We are required to work in this world, which is foreign to us, learning and being respectful of the local cultures and obeying the laws of this planet in each respective country all the while promoting good relationships with officials and protecting and keeping abreast of our fellow citizens.

Ambassadors protect their sovereign state's citizens living in a strange country while building and maintaining good diplomatic and economic ties with foreign nations and perform administrative duties for the embassy. The ambassador officially represents his country while stationed in a foreign land and represents his country to the other, an authorized diplomat sent by a country as its official representative to a foreign country.

In this case, those who accept Jesus as Lord, Master, Savior, and God receive accreditation after fully understanding all of God's Words. He is the one who authorized you to represent his interests. As ambassadors for Jesus, we are deciphering and projecting our home country of heaven's interests in this world. That is, to teach others who God really is and dispel myths, theories, and downright lies. We could find ourselves meeting and hosting politicians and even other evangelical diplomats. We will have to explain God's policies, as well as commands and laws that have been fulfilled by Christ to others, like Paul.

A certain amount of diplomacy will help individuals navigate various relationships professionally. These skills can include knowing when and how to change your communication style based on who you're speaking to and what you're discussing. It's best to engage in active listening, using positive words, phrases, and empathy statements. Having an awareness of cultural differences is fairly critical. Ambassadors can communicate in multiple languages. I only know a few who are helpful to break the uncomfortable silence between newbies.

Empathy

Ambassadors may spend time finding solutions for issues between their home and host countries or helping citizens from their home country overcome obstacles. When addressing these challenges, it helps if an ambassador can listen with compassion to understand the needs and concerns of everyone involved. An ambassador is also more likely to be successful if they find solutions that help everyone while respecting the customs and policies of their host country.

The first step in planting

First of all is the old real estate idiom: location, location, location. When you find a suitable and easily accessible building or home from which to start, then you can find some financial backers that are willing to finance your newly founded dreams of fulfilling God's word by being a "sower of the seed."

The City Network is an example of the place to start looking for a financial partner to help make your new church dreams come true. There are many such institutions that will finance and give guidance as to how to progress from a small church to a larger congregation as time and teaching line by line while remaining in context. But you have to watch out for the nightmares that are lurking around the corner. For example, a church was functioning normally on the outside, as far as the congregation was concerned, but then came the news that the pastor had been taking money from the church's accounts and spending it lavishly on himself and his wife. When this had come to light and the congregation demanded that the money be returned, the pastor and his wife fled and started charging the church for rent and back rent to which they had no right.

So now the church has rewritten their constitution in order to recover from the devastating blow to their confidence. As it is written in Matthew 7:15, "Beware of false prophets who come disguised as harmless sheep but are really vicious wolves." A wolf in sheep's clothing is someone who hides malicious intent under the guise of kindliness.

So which type of church to be like? I have been to many, and the experiences are just as varying. In the low church is the most fundamental teaching of God's Word and the most accurate, having baptism full immersion for an honest believer wanting to show the world his faith, the baptism of *professed believers only* to show they have washed away their faith in the world system. When I was baptized two years after Christ put his hand on me, I was fully aware that it was to show the church members that I had been fully immersed in Christ's death and resurrection.

Through baptism, you are counted by God as having died with Christ on the cross, been buried in the tomb with him, and raised from the dead with him.

True hearts

Jesus said to Peter, "Get thee behind me, Satan!", which is a quasi-equivalent of Jesus saying that Peter's heart and mind were being influenced by Satan.

Peter was trying to hold Jesus back from accomplishing his mission of saving all humanity from the second death, just as Satan, as a talking serpent, was able to get Eve to question God in the Garden of Eden.

Jesus has the power to see into people's hearts and minds. This I learned when I asked God to judge me. I have learned through what was taught in scripture about the unseen cross seen on the forehead of believers in Christ, as stated in Ezekiel 9:4.

The parable of the sower returns

A man went out to sow grain. The man represents a servant of God, and the seed is his message. Just as a planted seed starts to grow, the Word of God starts to deepen and grow within a person whose heart is not hardened by being trampled upon by the world. Take me, for example. When I rejected God outright at the age of ten, that was my age of accountability as I knew exactly what I was doing, or so I believed. My heart was as *hard as the path* the seeds fell on.

"Some seed fell on the path, and the birds ate it." The birds represent Satan and the influence of worldly pressure to reject God's Word. The seed on the path represents people who hear the message, but it is immediately lost. That was me exactly, from age ten to twenty-eight.

Some seed fell on rocky ground where there was little soil. The seed soon sprouted, but when the sun came up, it burnt the young plants, which are hope and giving glory to God. The seed on the rocky ground represents people who respond with initial enthusiasm, but the Word of God does not penetrate due to skepticism and internal dishonesty. When the hot sun of persecution from others or financial hard times pop up, they throw in the towel to douse the heat.

People in this category are initially attracted to the topic, like when I was an atheist listening to Billy Graham. I saw the huge crowds, heard his message, and was interested but then said, "Meh." My internal skepticism was hard at work extinguishing any interest in his message through a thought process bent on refusing a paradigm shift. In modern psychology, this is called a fatal flaw.

Now to where some seed fell among thornbushes, which grew up and choked the plants. The thornbushes choke the message of God. It is heard but caused the plants to die. Some people are too concerned with what fellow unbelievers think, like when I was about six and I was helping my mother with weeding in the front yard, I saw a weed that was coiling itself around the stem of a daisy, and it was crushing the daisy like a boa constrictor, much like unbelieving friends choking the life out of our hopes and dreams without us realizing it.

To continue, "some seed fell on good soil, and the plants produced corn." Good soil represents people who hear the message and live it in their lives. Some people have strong faith and remain dedicated to a Bible-directed lifestyle, even when things are difficult.

Sincerity vs. fakery

Most people I have talked to have walked away from secularism to faith in Christ because of a terrible train wreck in life, usually caused by drug, alcohol, or Californication lifestyles. None of this applies to me. I was a field service engineer for wet etch processing equipment with plenty of money coming in and was too Scrooge-minded to spend a dime of it on hobbies or habits that did not give an ROI. I was still driving the same 1973 Firebird Esprit to save even more money and because I loved that car.

Abraham was considered righteous by God because of his faith. By faith, you are sons and daughters of Abraham.

That is when I was challenged by the AOG pastor to ask God if what I had been taught is the truth and ask Jesus into my heart. When Christ appeared in my room and put his hand on me, that was a major paradigm shift for which I had no idea was coming.

So this is my opportunity to give back what has been given to me by God with such liberal generosity. Did I mention love? Love is still something that eludes me, a concept I have yet to fully grasp.

The teaching you need

As much as I did not want anything to do with the Bible for eighteen years, when Christ put his hand on me, I knew that I no longer had a choice. The next day, I started reading the Bible, and it was with great reluctance. But I do believe that the Holy Spirit was making sure that I read and accepted every word. And since then, I have read the KJV twice, the CJB five times, the Catholic Bible with the Apocrypha once, and the PEV until it fell apart. So I have a hunger for God's Word that I was in denial of, and it took three acts of God to get me to acknowledge it.

Get away from the cemetery, I mean the seminary college training, as it all too often teaches dead religion based on tradition. That is also why I am writing this chapter. Look at the apostle Paul and how he had zero seminary training. On the contrary, he was a pharisee of pharisees by his own admission, and they were caught up in a religion that was so over and above what God had given to Moses that it actually became a huge burden to the people.

2 Corinthians 3:5 says:

> It is not that we think we are qualified to do any-
> thing on our own. Our qualification comes from
> God.

If God calls you, he will provide for your needs as you progress. It all came from God, the Christ, and the Holy Spirit, plus revelations and spiritual manifestation. Seminary is often teaching replacement theology and denials of works of the Holy Spirit, which is tearing out pages from the Bible. Those who teach replacement theology have forgotten or deleted what Paul the apostle has said in Romans 11:1:

> I ask, then, has God rejected his people? By no
> means! For I myself am an Israelite, a descendant
> of Abraham, a member of the tribe of Benjamin.

The terms have to do with worship procedures, specifically the use of ritual, formula, clothing, and item themes in worship. Leaders of a high church congregation place a *high emphasis* on ceremony, clothes, and rituals. Leaders of a low church congregation place a *low emphasis* on such things and follow a free-ish worship style.

Anglican, Episcopal, Catholic, Orthodox, most Methodist and Lutheran, and some Presbyterian churches are considered high church. Baptist, Independent, Pentecostal, Quaker, Amish, some Methodist and Lutheran, and many Presbyterian churches are considered low church. Their worship services are characterized by congregational involvement, a relatively unstructured program, and an evangelical approach.

The distinction between high church and low church did not appear until after the Reformation. Then the question arose: as the Protestant church rejected the Roman Catholic doctrine, how much Catholic ritual can be retained? Let's look at church founders Martin Luther and Ulrich Zwingli, who went head to head on this issue.

Luther was like, as long as a rite was not specifically forbidden in the Bible, it was okay for the church to do it. Zwingli said that if a rite was not commanded or even mentioned in the New Testament, then it should not be practiced in the church at all.

What I have found that is correct in the worship of God at church is to open with music that praises God in the first person. The error of Job's friends is that they always referred to God in the third person, as a cipher, an entity that is distant, cold, and unfeeling. That is how to arouse God's anger, for he has proven over and over again in scripture, history, and my life that He is loving, close at times, constantly caring, and open to your prayers at all times.

Luther's position is called high church practice. Zwingli's view started the low church movement in the Westminster Confession:

> The acceptable way of worshiping the true God is instituted by himself, and so limited by his own revealed will, that he may not be worshiped according to the imaginations and devices of men, or the suggestions of Satan, under any visible representation or any other way not prescribed in the Holy Scripture.

Neither being high church nor low church guarantees the proper worship of God. As it says in John 4:24, "God is spirit, and his worshipers must worship *in the Spirit and in truth*."

I was not a member of any Christian church and yet saw what God hath done for me for worshiping him in Spirit and in truth. And if anyone loves and fears God, he is known by God. Send a soul call to God now as I first did. Gather together all the love you have for your family, friends, your memories, and your stuff and launch it like a catapult to him, who is on the throne in heaven, and wait patiently for his response. It will come. And remember what Jesus said in Matthew 10:41:

> The one who receives a prophet because he is a prophet will receive a prophet's reward, and the

one who receives a righteous person because he is a righteous person will receive a righteous person's reward.

So if you receive a prophet as one who speaks as an ambassador between you and the kingdom of God, you will be given the same reward as a prophet. To receive a righteous person would be like receiving Abraham himself into your house. So we are commanded to go out and fulfill the great commission in Matthew 28:18–20 from the CJB:

> Yeshua came and talked with them. He said, "All authority in heaven and on earth has been given to me. Therefore, go and make people from all nations into talmidim, immersing them into the reality of the Father, the Son and the Ruach HaKodesh, and teaching them to obey everything that I have commanded you. And remember! I will be with you always, yes, even until the end of the age."

The End

ABOUT THE AUTHOR

Mark Magill (https://fultonbooks.com) is a former Atheist transformed into a God-taught biblical studies enthusiast. For over twenty years, he has read through and researched different types of Bibles to become an expounder of scripture.

His work across multiple disciplines of electronics, aircraft, and field service engineering, to name a few, has given him a broad spectrum of the best of modern technology. Mark has served in the US Air Force over twenty years, in three technically challenging career fields.

He has also delved deeply into the biblical studies and the supernatural realm using a rare form of clearly defined spiritual discernment. This gives him a unique perspective in all things biblical and paranormal.